SPIRITUAL HEALING

A Handbook Of Activities, Guided Imagery, Meditations
And Prayers For Exploring And Enhancing
Our Own Spirituality And The Spirituality Of Others

SPIRITUAL HEALING

A Handbook Of Activities, Guided Imagery, Meditations
And Prayers For Exploring And Enhancing
Our Own Spirituality And The Spirituality Of Others

Douglas C. Smith
Theodore J. Chapin

P-S
P

Psycho-Spiritual Publications
Madison, Wisconsin

Douglas C. Smith
Psycho-Spiritual Publications
601 N. Segoe Road, Suite 305
Madison, Wisconsin 53705

Printed in the United States of America

ISBN 0-9672870-1-4

Contents

Do we not all have a right, not only to have our bodies treated with respect, but also, and perhaps even more important, our spirits? Spiritual care is not a luxury for a few; it is *the* essential right of every human being, as essential as political liberty, medical assistance, and equality of opportunity.

- Sogyal Rinpoche

Introduction

Thousands of health care professionals have been attending the seminars that I have been leading on caring for the sick, dying, and grieving. Each individual that attends one of these seminars writes an evaluation at the end of the presentation. The last question on that evaluation asks those attending to identify the one topic they would most want to have covered in future seminars. The overwhelming responses to that question read something like the following: "More on spiritual care!" "Spiritual care for people of different faiths." "Exploring and enhancing people's spirituality." "The importance of spirituality in health care." "Spiritual care for the dying and the bereaved." "Spiritual care! Spiritual care! And more spiritual care!" *Spiritual Healing* has been written to answer those requests.

Physicians, nurses, social workers, and clergy are making these requests because they have found that spirituality appears to be very important in a person's health, and many of their clientele are desiring to be treated in a holistic fashion, a fashion that takes into consideration their beliefs and values. Many people, health care professionals and their clientele, are realizing that a person's well-being involves the total person: physically, mentally, emotionally, and spiritually.

Also, all of us cannot help but be aware that in meeting anyone's spiritual needs we are often confronted with numerous forms of spirituality: various organized religions, schools of thought within each of those religions, various interpretations of those schools of thought, private spiritual opinions, individual philosophies of life, and eclectic combinations of any of the above. Any approach to someone's spiritual well-being must take into account the varieties of spiritual expressions.

Spiritual Healing is designed to enhance and strengthen the spirituality of the sick, dying, bereaved, and their caregivers as well as the general public. Much of the material in the book is purposefully designed so that it can be used with people of any religious, spiritual, or philosophical background. Also, all the material in the book is designed to be practical, workable tools: assessments, activities for spiritual explorations, guided imageries for spiritual enhancement, meditations, and prayers. This is what health care professionals and the general public appear to be needing, wanting, and demanding: a practical book on spirituality that can apply to all the major religions as well as any other form of spirituality. That is the intent of *Spiritual Healing*.

A good friend of mine, mentor, and spiritually-minded psychotherapist, Ted Chapin, has assisted me with the writing of this book. Ted's extensive practice in psychotherapy has been invaluable in adding to this collection of materials. We hope that you experience as much joy in doing your spiritual work as we have been experiencing in ours. Perhaps this material will help you on your journey as you help others on their journey.

Doug Smith

Activities For The Active Spirit

Chapter Introduction

As you read the first chapter you will discover many exercises intended to help yourself or another explore, engage, or express spiritual experiences in the midst of sickness, dying, bereavement, caregiving, or everyday life. Each exercise requests the participant to join in some type of inner exploration or outer activity. The benefits of these activities can be greatly enriched by sharing them with a trusted other who may act as a counselor or supportive guide. The role and style of the counselor is very important. While there are many ways to help others, one of the most effective styles is that of "facilitator" or active observer.

A facilitator is not passive, does not control the direction of the experience, and does not make judgements or conclusions about a participant's experience. A facilitator actively engages in the experience with the participant. As a facilitator you would observe the participant's thoughts, feelings, and reactions and respectfully help the participant reflect upon them. As a facilitator you would go with the ebb and flow of the process. You are at the same time willing to stop, take a sharp turn in an unexpected direction, or go deeper. You are comfortable with your own feelings and are willing to use them as a means to empathize and connect with the participant's experience. A facilitator has a strong sense of personal courage, faith, and commitment to his/her role and to the experiential process. As a facilitator you trust that the process is good and meaningful, whether or not it is pleasant or upsetting. You are honest in your own reactions and feelings and are willing to share them. You strive to be congruent in your interaction with the participant, for it is congruence, which allows the participant to trust the facilitator and to trust the process. Most important or all, you honor the participant's world view, whether or not you agree with it, or see it as healthy or not. A participant's world view is the structure by which the participant organizes his/her life and experience. It is the basis of a participants's security and requires the utmost of respect. In respecting a participant's world view, a facilitator is honoring another's values, roles, familiar language, history, important relationships, self-image, expectations, hopes, fears, duties and obligations, physical condition, energy, religiosity, and spirituality.

You are about to begin a sacred journey. You are about to witness your own or another's self-exploration, self-expression, and self-revelation. Be patient. Be respectful. Bring all of yourself to the experience. Treat it as a blessed event and neither you nor your companion will be disappointed.

SPIRITUAL ASSESSMENT:
A PERSON'S STRENGTH, PEACE, AND SECURITY

Intended Participant: The Sick, Dying, Bereaved, Caregivers, and/or General Public.

1. The participant would be asked to write down or verbalize answers to the following questions.

    A. Strength
        1. What is "strength" for you?
        2. Where can you go to get it?
        3. Who gives it to you?
        4. How can you get more?
    B. Peace
        1. What is "peace" for you?
        2. Where can you go to get it?
        3. Who gives it to you?
        4. How can you get more?
    C. Security
        1. What is "security" for you?
        2. Where can you go to get it?
        3. Who gives it to you?
        4. How can you get more?

2. A discussion over the above material could follow.

SPIRITUAL ASSESSMENT: MEANINGFUL SYMBOLS

Intended Participant: The Sick, Dying, Bereaved, Caregivers, and/or General Public.

1. The participant would be asked to gather 2-5 objects to place on a small table. These objects would symbolize what is most important in the person's life, what gives this person's life meaning and purpose, what this person most cherishes about his/her life. The objects could be described as "the glue" that holds the person's life together. The objects could also be described as a person's "spiritual vocabulary."

2. Possible objects could include:

   A. A book or books.
   B. A photograph or photographs.
   C. Religious objects.
   D. Mementos.
   E. Art work.
   F. Materials gathered from nature.
   G. A letter, letters, or other personal documents.

3. Discussion could follow with the person exploring why each item was chosen.

A Case Example From Doug

The above assessment was used with a woman named Alice. I gave the assignment to her one day while visiting her in her hospital room, saying that during my next visit I would be honored to see what she had placed on the table in her room. The next week I came back and discovered that she had cleared off the table and had only placed a single photograph on it, and nothing else. The photograph was of a German shepherd dog. Upon seeing only that photograph, I thought that perhaps she had not understood the assignment. Yet, I asked her why she had chosen that photograph, and only that photograph, to symbolize "the glue" that held her world together. How did that photograph of a dog represent her "spiritual vocabulary?"

She responded by saying that five years previously she had gone through a very messy divorce, and all the friends that she thought she had shared with her ex-husband sided with him, and no one sided with her. Everyone treated her differently the day after the divorce; everyone treated her as if she was somehow a less valuable person after that divorce. Well, everyone except for her dog, her German shepherd dog, who loved her the same the day after the divorce as the day before the divorce, who treated her as being the very same person she had always been. She said, "Doug. If you want to talk to me about religion, or anything like that, you talk to me in those terms: that unconditional love that I found that dog having for me which no one else had for me."

I think she understood the assignment quite well. Imagine the conversation we could have given that "spiritual vocabulary." That single photograph revealed much about Alice's agenda for spiritual healing.

SPIRITUAL ASSESSMENT: WORD ASSOCIATION

Intended Participant: The Sick, Dying, Bereaved, Caregivers, and/or General Public.

1. The participant would be asked to write down or verbalize the first word that comes to mind after hearing each of the following words:

> "God."
> "Minister."
> "Evil."
> "Scripture."
> "Prayer."
> "Death."
> "Nature."
> "Worship."
> "Heaven."
> "Love."

2. A discussion between the person assessing and the person being assessed could follow. The person being assessed would begin the discussion by guessing why he/she came up with each of the responses.

SPIRITUAL ASSESSMENT:
YOU ARE PRESIDENT OF THE BOARD OF DIRECTORS

Intended Participant: The Sick, Dying, Bereaved, Caregivers,
and/or General Public.

1. The participant would be given the following scenario:
"Imagine that you are the president of the board of directors of
the largest religious building in your community. You can direct
how that building is used and what the staff do."

> A. "How would that building be used if it were
> promoting your values/theology? What activities would
> occur there on an average week?"
> B. "How would that staff be best employed? What would
> that staff be doing on an average week?"

2. Discussion could follow.

SPIRITUAL ASSESSMENT:
YOU ARE DEAN OF THE SEMINARY

Intended Participant: The Sick, Dying, Bereaved, Caregivers, and/or General Public.

1. The participant would be given the following scenario: "Imagine that you are the dean of a seminary. You get to determine four required courses for every seminarian. What would those four required courses be?"

Examples:
A. Preaching 101
B. Meeting The Needs Of The Poor 101
C. Conflict Management 101
D. Remembering Names 101

2. Discussion could follow.

SPIRITUAL ASSESSMENT: EXPLORATORY QUESTIONS

Intended Participant: The Sick, Dying, Bereaved, Caregivers, and/or General Public.

1. The participant would be asked to write down or verbalize his/her answers to the following questions:

> A. "How would you describe your basic philosophy or belief system? In other words, what is the 'glue' that holds your world together?"
> B. "How would you describe your purpose in living? In other words, what do you believe is the best thing that you can do with your life?"
> C. "Do you believe that there is a force or a being responsible for the creating and sustaining of our existence? If so, why? If not, why not?"
> D. "How would you describe who or what you were before you were born?"
> E. "How would you describe who or what you will be after you die?"

2. Discussion could follow.

OBJECT MEDITATION

Intended Participant: The Sick, Dying, Bereaved, Caregivers, and/or General Public.

1. Any object that elicits comfort can be the focus of a daily meditation. A possible object might be a crucifix, a statue of the Buddha, a mandala, a menorah, a copy of the Koran, a flower, a family photograph, a stone, a candle.

2. The participant would spend about 15-20 minutes centering all of his/her attention upon this object of comfort. Whenever other thoughts intrude, the participant could close his/her eyes and then open them up again upon the object of concentration.

3. With every intake of breath, the person could imagine breathing in the essence of the object. With every breath expelled, the person could imagine breathing out all that is not attuned with the object.

THE WOUNDED HEALER RESUME

Intended Participant: The Sick, Dying, Bereaved, Caregivers, and/or General Public.

1. Construct a resume based upon your past and present wounds problems, pain and suffering, disabilities, shortcomings.

2. First list your major past and present wounds: problems, pain and suffering, disabilities, shortcomings.

3. Then, after each item on the list, write how that item makes you a better person. Sample exploratory questions:

> A. "How does that item equip you to better handle your future wounds?"
> B. "How does that item help you to better understand, and address, the wounds of others?"
> C. "How does that item improve you in qualities like strength, courage, endurance, faithfulness, and hope?"

4. Finally write the resume in a formal form, just like a regular resume.

NAMING THE PAIN

Intended Participant: The Sick, Dying, Bereaved, Caregivers, and/or General Public.

1. Within many spiritual and religious traditions the naming or renaming of something is the same as mastering that thing. The participant would meditate upon this concept.

2. The participant would then bring to mind his/her greatest pain. After the participant has meditated upon this pain, he/she would verbalize an appropriate name for the pain.

3. Then the participant would imagine the pain having a physical shape. After that has been imagined, the participant would verbalize what that shape would be.

4. Then the participant would imagine the pain as a color and name that color.

5. Then the participant would imagine the pain as a sound and name that sound.

6. Then the participant would imagine the shape he/she would like the pain to be, visualizing in his/her mind the original shape changing into this new shape (2-3 minutes).

7. Then the participant would imagine the color he/she would like the pain to be, visualizing in his/her mind the original color changing into this new color (2-3 minutes).

8. Then the participant would imagine the sound he/she would like the pain to be, imagining the original sound changing into this new sound (2-3 minutes).

9. Then the participant would rename the transformed pain with an appropriate name for its transformed state.

10. Whenever the pain comes back in its original form, the participant could call it by its original name then begin transforming it until he/she can call it by its new name.

SHOWING SOME SPIRITUAL MUSCLE

Intended Participant: The Sick, Dying, Bereaved, Caregivers, and/or General Public.

1. Choose a muscle group that you would like to improve (stomach muscles, buttocks, or leg muscles).

2. As soon as someone comes into your presence with negative energy (energy that you are receiving in a negative way), internally thank that person for coming into your presence and providing you with a potential positive gift.

3. While that person is exuding that negative energy, use that energy to tighten and loosen, tighten and loosen, tighten and loosen your chosen muscle group. Do this in such a manner so that the person has no idea what you are doing. (You can even be talking to this person while you are tightening and loosening your muscles.)

4. When the person has finished giving you that negative energy (which you have converted into positive energy), internally thank the person for coming into your presence and hope that he/she might soon return to give you more gifts of energy so that you can further improve yourself.

JOYS AND CONCERNS ALTAR

Intended Participant: The Sick, Dying, Bereaved, Caregivers, and/or General Public.

1. The participant would designate a place in his/her home (coffee table, end table, top of a dresser) to be a "Joys And Concerns Altar." The participant would then place two candles on the altar: a candle for concerns and a candle for joys. At regular intervals (every evening, every Sunday evening) the two candles would be lit with a dedication and a meditation.

2. The "candle for concerns" is lit first with the participant dedicating it to a particular worry, pain, petition, or hope that he/she has had during the day or week. The participant then meditates for 3-5 minutes on that worry, pain, petition, or hope.

3. The "candle for joys" is then lit with the participant dedicating it to a particular peace of mind, happiness, or pleasure that was had during the day or week. The participant then meditates for 3-5 minutes on that peace of mind, happiness, or pleasure.

SPIRITUAL EXPLORATIONS
BASED ON TAOIST THOUGHT

Intended Participant: The Sick, Dying, Bereaved, Caregivers, and/or General Public.

1. A participant would rewrite the following quotations using his/her own words rather than the words of the text, trying to duplicate the text's meaning but in different words. This rewriting will help the participant incorporate the meaning of the quotations.

2. Although the following quotations come from a Taoist tradition (from the book The Way of Lao Tzu), the person doing the rewriting does not have to be a Taoist.

A. "Manifest plainness,
   Embrace simplicity,
   Reduce selfishness,
   Have few desires."
B. "The softest things in the world overcome the hardest things in the world."
C. "I treat those who are good with goodness,
   And I also treat those who are not good with goodness.
   Thus goodness is attained."
D. "He who knows the eternal is all-embracing."

3. The rewritten statements could then be discussed, having some of the conversation center around how these rewritten statements might relate to the person's current circumstances.

SPIRITUAL EXPLORATIONS
BASED ON CHRISTIAN THOUGHT

Intended Participant: The Sick, Dying, Bereaved, Caregivers, and/or General Public.

1. A participant would rewrite the following quotations, using his/her own words rather than the words of the text, trying to duplicate the text's meaning but in different words. This rewriting will help the participant incorporate the meaning of the quotations.

2. Although the following quotations come from a Christian tradition (from the New American Standard Bible), the person doing the rewriting does not have to be a Christian:

> A. "Whoever exalts himself shall be humbled; and whoever humbles himself shall be exalted."
> B. "Draw near to God and He will draw near to you."
> C. "Whether we are awake or asleep, we may live together with Him."
> D. "Rejoice always."

3. The rewritten statements could then be discussed, having some of the conversation center around how these rewritten statements might relate to the person's current circumstances.

SPIRITUAL EXPLORATIONS
BASED ON HINDU THOUGHT

Intended Participant: The Sick, Dying, Bereaved, Caregivers, and/or General Public.

1. A participant would rewrite the following quotations using his/her own words rather than the words of the text, trying to duplicate the text's meaning but in different words. This rewriting will help the participant incorporate the meaning of the quotations.

2. Although the following quotations come from a Hindu tradition (from the book The Ten Principal Upanishads), the person doing the rewriting does not have to be Hindu:

> A. "He who gives with purity, gets purity in return; he who gives with passion, gets passion in return; he who gives with ignorance, gets ignorance in return."
> B. "The man who can see all creatures in himself, himself in all creatures, knows no sorrow."
> C. "Spirit is everywhere, upon the right, upon the left, above, below, behind, in front. What is the world but Spirit?"
> D. "From joy all things are born, by joy they live, toward joy they move, into joy they return."

3. The rewritten statements could then be discussed, having some of the conversation center around how these rewritten statements might relate to the person's current circumstances.

SPIRITUAL EXPLORATIONS
BASED ON BUDDHIST THOUGHT

Intended Participant: The Sick, Dying, Bereaved, Caregivers, and/or General Public.

1. A participant would rewrite the following quotations using his/her own words rather than the words of the text, trying to duplicate the text's meaning but in different words.

2. Although the following quotations come from a Buddhist tradition (from the book The Teaching Of Buddha), the person doing the rewriting does not have to be a Buddhist.

> A. "Human beings tend to move in the direction of their thoughts. If they harbor greedy thoughts, they become more greedy; if they think angry thoughts, they become more angry; if they hold foolish thoughts, their feet move in that direction."
> B. "Each man has a different view of things according to the state of his mind. Some people see the city where they live as fine and beautiful, others see it as dirty and dilapidated. It all depends on the state of their minds."
> C. "Buddha does not always appear as a Buddha. Sometimes He appears as an incarnation of evil, sometimes as a woman, a god, a king, or a statesman; sometimes He appears in a brothel or in a gambling house."
> D. "Buddhahood fills everything."

3. The rewritten statements could then be discussed, having some of the conversation center around how these rewritten statements might relate to the person's current circumstances.

SPIRITUAL EXPLORATIONS
BASED ON JEWISH THOUGHT

Intended Participant: The Sick, Dying, Bereaved, Caregivers, and/or General Public.

1. A participant would rewrite the following quotations using his/her own words rather than the words of the text, trying to duplicate the text's meaning but in different words.

2. Although the following quotations come from a Jewish tradition (from the Tanakh), the person doing the rewriting does not have to be Jewish:

> A. "When you call Me, and come and pray to Me, I will give heed to you. You will search for Me and find Me, if only you seek Me wholeheartedly."
> B. "Cast your burden on the Lord and He will sustain you."
> C. "The Lord is my light and my help; whom should I fear?
>   The Lord is the stronghold of my life, whom should I dread?"
> D. "Though I walk through a valley of deepest darkness, I fear no harm, for You are with me;
>   Your rod and Your staff - they comfort me."

3. The rewritten statements could then be discussed, having some of the conversation center around how these rewritten statements might relate to the person's current circumstances.

CELEBRATING LIFE

Intended Participant: The Sick, Dying, Bereaved, Caregivers, and/or General Public.

1. The participant spends 5 minutes just being mindful of his/her breathing.

2. The participant spends 5 minutes viewing, feeling, and smelling a flower.

3. The participant spends 5 minutes viewing, feeling, smelling, and slowly chewing a piece of bread.

4. The participant spends 20 minutes slowly making a cup of coffee or tea, smelling it, sipping it, and feeling it flow throughout his/her body.

5. The participant spends 10 minutes doing a creative dance that expresses his/her feelings after doing all the above activities

6. The participant spends a total of 5 minutes examining his/her face in a mirror, feeling its various features. The fourth minute is spent frowning and the last minute smiling.

CLEANSING CEREMONY

Intended Participant: The Sick, Dying, Bereaved, Caregivers, and/or General Public.

1. As a prelude to this activity, you might want to expend some physical energy. What is done to expend that energy could be appropriately matched to your mood and physical abilities (running, cleaning, pillow hitting, isometric exercises, stretching).

2. You would prepare a warm bath. Epsom salts, herbs, or oils could be added to the water.

3. In the bathroom, the lighting might be dimmed. Candles could be lit and incense could be burned.

4. Your favorite music could be playing in the background. A recording of sounds from nature might be preferred.

5. Before entering the bath, you might want to say some prayer like the following: "I take this bath so that I might be renewed. May I experience complete relaxation. May my mind and body be soothed. May my spirit be awakened. I take this bath so that I might be renewed."

6. Try to spend at least 20 minutes in the bath. To assure your continuing comfort, hot water could be periodically added to keep the bath water warm.

DEDICATING ONESELF TO LIVING A SACRED LIFE

Intended Participant: The Sick, Dying, Bereaved, Caregivers, and/or General Public.

1. The participant would take a candle, a bowl of water, and some incense to a quiet, isolated place.

2. After lighting the candle and the incense, the participant would take 10 minutes to fully examine his/her surroundings: being conscious of breathing in the quietness of the place, breathing in the light of the candle, and breathing in the fragrance of the incense.

3. The participant would then dip some fingers in the bowl of water and touch the wetness to his/her forehead, saying, "I bless my mind and my understanding. May my thoughts be focused on all that is good and pure in this life."

4. The participant would then dip some fingers in the bowl of water and touch the wetness to his/her ears, saying, "I bless my ears and my hearing. May I strive to hear all that is good and pure in this life."

5. The participant would then dip some fingers in the bowl of water and touch the wetness to his/her eyes, saying, "I bless my eyes and my seeing. May I strive to see all that is good and pure in this life."

6. The participant would then dip some fingers in the bowl of water and touch the wetness to his/her lips, saying, "I bless my lips and my speaking. May I strive to say only what is good and pure, only that which can be for the benefit of others."

7. The participant would then wash his/her hands in the bowl of water, saying, "I bless my hands and my doing. May I strive to do only what is good and pure, only that which can be for the benefit of others."

8. The participant would then reflect for 10 minutes on the words that were spoken.

GIVEAWAY CEREMONY

Intended Participant: The Dying, Bereaved, and Their Caregivers.

1. The giving away of a person's possessions can take on additional meaning when done in a group setting. The giving away can be done by the dying person before he/she dies or by the executor (or other designated person) after the death.

2. The planning of the event as well as the holding of the event can be very therapeutic.

3. Invitations for the event would be sent out to all the people who would be receiving a gift.

4. As each item is given away, special memories of the item would be shared and reasons would be given for why the particular item was going to a particular recipient.

5. Each recipient could then give some response of gratitude.

A DYING PERSON'S SPIRITUAL AFFIRMATIONS

Intended Participant: Dying Person.

1. Any of the following affirmations could be repeated verbally or internally each day: first thing in the morning and last thing at night.

2. Encourage the participant to pick his/her own affirmation.

3. A participant's chosen affirmation could be visibly posted as a physical reminder of the verbal or internal practice, posting the affirmation on a mirror, refrigerator door, or some other frequently visited location.

4. Sample affirmations:

> A. I will soon be in the arms of God.
> B. God's love has been intended for me.
> C. I am getting closer and closer to God.
> D. Soon there will be no barriers between me and God.
> E. Make room for me, God. I am coming.
> F. This is a day that God has made. I will rejoice and be glad in it.

5. The word "God" is used in these affirmations, but that word can be substituted with the words "Jesus," "the Revered Buddha," "Allah," "the Goddess," "the Divine Spirit," or any other appropriate wording.

MY SPIRITUAL TRAVELOGUE

Intended Participant: Dying Person.

1. The dying person would purchase a bound book of blank pages. The book would be divided into three sections, one entitled "Thoughts on God" or "Thoughts On The Existence Of A Reality Greater Than Myself," one entitled "Thoughts On My Value And Lack Of Value As A Person," and one entitled "Thoughts On Afterlife."

2. The dying person would make a dated entry in at least one of the sections each day.

3. This participant would then periodically share the contents of his/her journal with a trusted friend.

A DYING PERSON'S DREAM JOURNAL

Intended Participant: Dying Person.

1. The dying person could create a journal of all of his/her memorable dreams, especially those in which the subject of death is somehow present.

2. After recording the dream, the participant would address in the journal the following three questions:

> A. What message is there in the dream that might have relevance to my past, especially in regards to any "unfinished business" I might have: something I needed to do but have yet to do, someone with whom I have needed to speak but have yet to, etc.?
> B. What message is there in the dream that might have relevance for my present? Is there something I need to be doing now that I am not? Is there something I am not doing now that I need to do?
> C. What message is there in the dream that might have relevance for my future, especially related to what my priorities might need to be?

LETTER FROM MY HIGHER SELF

Intended Participant: Dying Person.

1. Soon after a person has been informed of his or her terminal prognosis, that person would write a list of all the compliments he/she has received from family members, friends, and associates. Next, this person would write a list of some of his/her favorite life accomplishments.

2. The material in these two lists would then be put in the form of a letter addressed to the person. At the bottom of the letter would be the words "yours truly." The dying person would then sign his/her name under the salutation. This is a letter written to the participant from the participant.

3. The letter would then be placed in an envelope with the participant's name on the outside of the envelope.

4. The letter would then be given to a trusted family member or friend of the participant with the instructions that the letter would be delivered if the participant would ever be in a state of mind where he/she was questioning the value of his/her life.

A BEREAVED PERSON'S SPIRITUAL AFFIRMATIONS

Intended Participant: Bereaved Person.

1. Any of the following affirmations could be repeated verbally or internally each day.

2. Encourage the participant to pick his/her own affirmation.

3. A participant's chosen affirmation could be visibly posted as a physical reminder of the verbal or internal practice, posting the affirmation on a mirror, refrigerator door, or some other frequently visited location.

4. Sample affirmations:

> A. I receive strength through the comfort of God. I receive comfort through the strength of God.
> B. Although clouds of loss and despair might enter my world, I know that the light of God can never disappear.
> C. I will take a day at a time knowing that God is with me when the sun rises and will not desert me when the sun sets.
> D. God was with me yesterday. God is with me today. God will be with me tomorrow.
> E. God's love is behind me. God's love is before me. God's love is in me.

5. The word "God" is used in these affirmations, but you can substitute "Jesus," "the Revered Buddha," "Allah," "the Goddess," "the Divine Spirit," or any other appropriate wording.

FAREWELL GIFTS

Intended Participant: Bereaved Person.

1. Before the burial of the deceased, each family member of the deceased could choose an object to place in the casket:

> A. A personal possession of the family member.
> B. A letter from the family member to the deceased person listing (and giving thanks for) all that the family member has received from the deceased.
> C. A special photograph taken of the deceased person and the family member together.
> D. A symbolic item representing something about the relationship between the family member and the deceased.

2. The objects could be placed in the casket by the person who is giving the object, or all objects could be collected and given to a member of the mortuary's staff to place in the casket.

3. Each family member could later explain how he/she came to choose the particular object that was placed in the casket and what it meant for them.

RITUAL WHEN NOT BEING PRESENT AT A FUNERAL

Intended Participant: Bereaved Person.

1. The participant could say a prayer or read through a funeral service liturgy at the same time that the actual funeral service is in progress.

2. The participant could light a candle in his/her home or at a place of worship during the day of the funeral.

3. He/she could get a photograph of the person who has died and talk to the photograph, saying everything he/she always wanted to say but never did.

4. He/she could write a long letter to the person who has died, writing everything he/she always wanted to say but never did.

5. He/she could spend half an hour in silent reflection about memories of the deceased person, reflecting also upon any of the above activities that might have been done.

6. The participant could plant a tree, shrub, or flower in a special place shared with the person who has died.

MEMORY BOOK

Intended Participant: Bereaved Person.

1. The participant could design and fill a scrapbook in memory of the loved one.

2. The cover of the book could be made from some special material (a former article of clothing, a favorite pattern of the person who has died).

3. The book could hold several items:

> A. Birth certificate.
> B. Various photographs.
> C. Matchbook covers or menus from favorite restaurants.
> D. Reminders of vacations taken.
> E. Person's favorite passages from literature or scripture.
> F. Newspaper announcements (birth, school events, marriage, retirement, etc.).
> G. Letters sent and received.
> H. Funeral service program.
> I. Sympathy cards.

4. If an entire family is doing the project, each family member could be responsible for gathering materials from a particular time in the person's life or from a particular role the person had (father, husband, businessman, golfer, community activist, etc.).

5. Every other page could be blank. The blank pages would be used in the future to make comments (thoughts, feelings, additional remembrances) when reviewing the book.

6. The book could be placed in a special place.

PRIVATE SERVICE OF REMEMBRANCE

Intended Participant: Bereaved Person.

1. In addition to the public funeral service, a person might want to have a special service at home the same day as the public service or the following weekend or at the one month anniversary. This service would just be for the family and/or really close friends.

2. The theme and disposition of the service (celebratory, meditative, humorous, solemn) would be known by all attending prior to the service.

3. The service could be preceded or followed by a meal.

4. Each person attending could give a short presentation (eulogy, reading, poem, musical piece).

5. Pictures and mementos could be placed all around the room where the service is held.

MEMORIAL GARDEN

Intended Participant: Bereaved Person

1. Select a location for planting a memorial garden.

2. Meditate upon your relationship with the deceased and design the garden in a manner which symbolizes your relationship.

3. Select the plantings you wish to use and prepare a garden bed. Remember that you can shape the garden any way you like. You can include meaningful elements such as rocks, statues, and bird baths.

4. Plant the garden while reflecting upon the beginning of your relationship.

5. Water and fertilize the garden reflecting upon who your relationship was nurtured.

6. Go back to the garden in the fall and meditate upon the dying plants.

7. Prepare the garden for winter by cutting the dead plants and covering the ground for winter.

8. Return in spring and observe the new growth. Meditate upon how your own life has been reshaped by the loss of the deceased and notice the new growth which has begun.

A Case Example From Ted

It had been 25 years since Helen, my mother-in-law, lost her husband, R.W. (Bill) to cancer. She, my wife Lori, and her brother and sister, Donald and Debi, had gone on to have very fulfilling and productive lives. However when the 25th anniversary of Bill's death approached, they all felt the need to commemorate the date with something special. They decided to design and plant a memorial garden.

They selected a small, vacant lot on the main street of their hometown. They planted trees, bushes, and flowering plants. A winding path, flag pole, and ornate cement benches were put in place to allow passers-by the opportunity to sit down, rest their feet, and enjoy the garden. A brass memorial plaque was installed with R.W.'s name, dates of life, and a short reflection.

Helen, her neighbors, her children, and her children's families frequent the garden whenever they get a chance. They water the flowers, prune the bushes, and even clean the plaque and the benches as an act of love and continuing memorial.

LETTING GO RITUAL

Intended Participant: Bereaved Person.

1. Before the ritual begins the bereaved person selects an object which symbolizes the deceased. This object could be a piece of clothing, picture, or any possession of the deceased.

2. Then the object is taken to a special place the deceased and the bereaved enjoyed together.

3. A hole is then dug in the ground or a fire pit prepared for a ritualistic burial or burning of the object.

4. A short meditation is offered before the object is buried or burnt.

5. The object is then buried or burned.

6. The bereaved meditates upon letting the object and the deceased go.

FEELING STONES

Intended Participant: Bereaved Person.

1. Find several differently shaped and colored stones which somehow reflect your different emotional states: sadness, loss, anger, relief, guilt, love, calm, peacefulness.

2. Take a particular stone in your hand. Hold it snugly.

3. Meditate upon the emotion you are feeling. Let the feeling build inside you. When you feel it at its fullest measure, strongly huff the air out of your lungs through your nose and imagine the emotion flowing from your hand into the stone.

4. Repeat the exercise for any emotion you like.

5. If you later want to recover a lost feeling, simply pick up the stone, and feel it in your hand. If needed, you can also meditate upon the last emotion.

6. Keep your feeling stones as long as you like. When you feel finished with them, put them in a special place or use the 'Letting Go Ritual' (on previous page) to dispose of them.

ANNIVERSARY SERVICE OF REMEMBRANCE

Intended Participant: Bereaved Person.

1. At the one year anniversary of the death, a minister (or other special person) could lead a special memorial service.

2. Appropriate readings, prayers and/or music, might be chosen by the bereaved person.

3. The bereaved person might want to personally choose some people to have certain parts in the service: a way of enhancing service and honoring some of those attending.

PILGRIMAGE OF REMEMBRANCE

Intended Participant: Bereaved Person.

1. A bereaved person could set aside some time (a long weekend, a week) to visit a place his/her loved one really appreciated (a vacation site, a former place of residence).

2. The bereaved person could spend some silent reflection time in a restaurant, building, and/or outdoor location where his/her loved one might have frequented.

3. Before leaving this pilgrimage site to return home, the bereaved person could leave something to the community in remembrance of the person who has died (a book purchased and inscribed for a local library, a memorial tree planted at a special place, some flowers for a church or synagogue).

4. The bereaved person could then try to share some of the experiences from the pilgrimage with a friend.

A Case Example From Doug

I did my own pilgrimage of remembrance twelve years after the death of my daughter Kristin. I was in graduate school at the time, studying counseling at Bradley University in Peoria, Illinois, the city in which my daughter had died. I took a day off from studying to do the pilgrimage.

I started the day in the intensive care center for infants at St. Francis Hospital (where Kristin had died). I spent some time looking through glass walls at infants attached to various life-supporting machines; I recalled visions of Kristin as she was attached to similar machines. I spent an hour sitting in a waiting room reflecting upon the day I had waited for Kristin's open heart surgery to end. I walked the halls reflecting upon the times I had walked those very halls twelve years ago.

At the end of the morning I went down to the gift shop and bought some flowers. I took the flowers up to one of the nurses' stations in that intensive care center and left them on a desk. Attached to the flowers was a note: "In thanksgiving for all the good work that you have done and all that you will do in the future. Kristin."

After eating in the hospital cafeteria, where I had eaten so many meals those many years ago, I went over to the office of Dr. Albers (the surgeon who had operated on Kristin and had provided invaluable emotional support for me after her death). He graciously met with me as we reviewed the time we had shared together. I expressed my thanks and hugged him as I left.

I then went to the church columbarium where Kristin's ashes were. I sat in the church, recalling her funeral and all the nice things people had done for me at that time. I gave a prayer of thanksgiving for all those who had cared for me. I also gave a prayer of thanksgiving for the gift of Kristin.

The next day I had an appointment with the counselor I was seeing on a regular basis. She listened as I reviewed all the feelings I had experienced on my pilgrimage of remembrance. I felt much sadness and did some crying, but I also felt very good for having done that pilgrimage; it was a very important step in my ongoing growth with, and through, my daughter Kristin; it felt like a kind of spiritual cleansing. I have come to look at that pilgrimage of remembrance as a necessary step back in time in order to help me make a healthful step forward in time.

RIVER OF LIFE

Intended Participant: Bereaved Person.

1. Locate a quiet stream or a meandering river.

2. Create, or take with you, an object which symbolizes your relationship with the deceased.

3. Hold the object in your hand while you meditate upon the stream and your relationship.

4. When you are ready, drop the object into the stream or river.

5. Watch the object's movement along with the river's current.

6. Notice the obstacles it encounters as it passes along the waterway.

7. Notice the beauty of its free flowing movement as it slips further out of sight.

8. Meditate upon the eventual destination of the object as it takes nature's course.

ALTAR OF REMEMBRANCE

Intended Participant: Bereaved Person.

1. The bereaved person could designate a place in his/her home (coffee table, end table, top of a dresser) to be an "Altar of Remembrance." This could be a place of periodic reflection or simply an ever-present reminder of the ongoing presence and influence of the loved one.

2. On the altar, there could be several items:

A. An altar cloth could be made from some of the person's clothing (a scarf, cloth cut from a favorite outfit).
B. Photographs of person (different periods in person's life).
C. A ring, watch, or other piece of jewelry.
D. A reminder of a favorite hobby (a model train car for a model train enthusiast, a kitchen utensil for a cook, a golf ball for a golfer, a favorite book for a reader).
E. A framed birth (or marriage) certificate.
F. Favorite passages from scripture or other favorite quotations.
G. A laminated obituary notice.
H. A candle to burn on the loved one's birthdays, on anniversaries, or on holidays.
I. A flower or plant.

ALTERNATIVE HOLIDAY RITUALS

Intended Participant: Bereaved Person.

1. On holidays or special anniversaries, instead of trying to duplicate the traditional routines (which carry with them memories that might only produce sadness), you could start a new ritual.

2. Here are some possibilities:

> A. Take a day to watch videos, watching 2-4 movies staring a favorite actress or actor.
> B. Go on a day trip with a friend. The friend could have also recently lost someone.
> C. Serve a holiday meal in a soup kitchen.
> D. Start a redecorating project in the home.
> E. Plant a tree, some flowers, or some vegetables.
> F. A favorite book could be reread each year, beginning on the day of this holiday.

HOLIDAY TABLECLOTH

Intended Participant: Bereaved Person.

1. Every holiday meal, all the members of a family would sign their names on a special tablecloth. The names could later be embroidered on the tablecloth

2. Every holiday meal the tablecloth is used, showing the names of everyone in the past who has sat at the table.

3. Before beginning the meal, there would be a silent meditation, remembering those who have previously sat at the table.

THE FIRST CHRISTMAS AFTER A DEATH

Intended Participant: Bereaved Person.

1. Each bereaved family member would think of one of the favorite gifts he/she has received from the departed person. The gift could be tangible or intangible.

2. Each family member would then write the name of that gift on a piece of paper, putting it in a box, and then wrapping it up.

3. The gifts from the departed person would be either the first or last gifts opened on Christmas morning.

4. Upon opening the gift, each family member would read aloud what they had written.

REWARD YOURSELF

Intended Participant: Bereaved Person.

1. The bereaved person would bring to mind how he/she could be functioning a lot worse than is currently the case.

2. The participant could then choose a reward to acknowledge his/her good job at coping.

    A. A massage.
    B. A new outfit or pair of shoes.
    C. An uplifting play, musical, or concert.
    D. An out of town retreat.
    E. A course at a local community college, YMCA, or YWCA.
    F. A trip to visit a friend.
    G. A mindful book to read.

FORGIVING THE PERSON WHO HAS DIED

Intended Participant: Bereaved Person.

1. The participant would acquire three pieces of colored paper: a yellow one, a red one, and a green one. On one side of the yellow piece of paper, the participant would write all the things the person who has died did that caused sadness for the participant. On one side of the red piece of paper, the participant would write all the things that person did that caused him/her to be angry. On one side of the green one, the participant would write all the other things that person did that caused any other kind of hurt.

2. Placing his/her hands on the three pieces of paper, the participant would read the following: "_____, I forgive you for all the times you have made me sad. _____, I forgive you for all the times you have made me angry. _____, I forgive you for all the times you have hurt me. _____, I forgive you. I too have been less than perfect. I too probably caused you sadness, anger, and hurt. I love you and I want to remember you for all the good you have done and all the love that you have shown to me. And life will always have sadness, anger, and hurt. I need to learn from it and grow from it, and I must somehow come to an understanding of how I need to go on learning and growing. I forgive you. I forgive you. I forgive you. I love you. I love you. I love you. And I must go on, somehow learning and growing from sadness, anger, and hurt."

3. The participant would then turn the three pieces of paper over and cut the paper so as to form a flower. The yellow piece of paper would be cut in the shape of a circle for the center of a flower. The red piece of paper would be cut in the shape of flower petals. A stem and leaves would be made from the green piece of paper.

4. The participant would then paste the pieces of paper on a large sheet of white paper, pasting the written sides down.

5. Finally, the flower is mounted on a refrigerator door or other prominent place as a reminder to the participant of his/her forgiveness of the person who has died.

RITUAL OF SELF-FORGIVENESS

Intended Participant: Bereaved Person.

1. Get three pieces of colored paper: a yellow one, a red one, and a green one. On one side of the yellow one, write all the things that you did that might have made the departed person sad. On one side of the red one, write all the things you did that might have made the loved one angry. On one side of the green one, write all the other things that you did that might have hurt the loved one.

2. Placing your hands on the three pieces of paper, read the following: "I am just human and I have made mistakes. We all do. Yet, I have tried hard to do my best. And I must try to remember the good things that I did and not be overly troubled by my mistakes. I forgive myself for my mistakes. I forgive myself. I forgive myself. I forgive myself. I have intended good. And I have done much good. And I am good."

3. You would then turn the three pieces of paper over and cut the paper so as to form a flower, the flower's center made of yellow, petals of red, stem and leaves of green.

4. You would then paste the pieces of paper on a large sheet of white paper, pasting the written side down.

5. Finally, the flower is mounted on a refrigerator door or other prominent place as a reminder of the forgiveness.

RESOLVING GUILT

Intended Participant: Bereaved Person.

1. Reflect upon your feelings of guilt.

> A. What do you wish you had done but didn't do?
> B. What do you wish you had said but didn't say?
> C. What do you wish you could do over?
> D. What do you regret that feels like it can never be undone?

2. Meditate upon you penance for your behavior.

> A. What can you now do for yourself or someone else?
> B. What can you now say loud and clear?
> C. What can you now do over for someone else?
> D. What can you do now to make up for your deepest regret?

3. Commit yourself to some specific action.

4. As you commence the action, meditate upon the fulfillment of your penance.

5. Thank the deceased person for the opportunity to learn from the guilt you felt with him/her.

A Case Example From Ted

I remember my first significant experience with guilt. I was a sophomore in high school. Like other teenagers, I was active in sports and had many friends. Most of my friendships were casual, as was the case with John.

John was a nice kid. His parents were professional people in town and he had several brothers and sisters. I used to have a brief conversation with John just about every day before classes started. One day I noticed John wasn't at school. Later that morning an announcement was made that John had died. I later learned through the newspaper that he had committed suicide. I felt awful. If only I had talked to him more. He didn't seem that upset to me. Maybe I should have been more of a friend to him. He obviously needed one. If I had been more of a friend, maybe this wouldn't have happened. I felt shameful and sad that somehow, I had let him down.

Reflecting on those days now, I suspect that my experience with John's suicide is one of several events that helped me decide to become a therapist. While I still regret John's death, I continue to honor his spirit by helping others with their depression and suicidal feelings. John motivated me to learn how to have much deeper and more meaningful relationships with others. I'm certain that my family, friends, and clients have benefitted too. Thank you John.

MEMORIAL QUILT

Intended Participant: Bereaved Person.

1. The project is to make a quilt with each square representing either a special time in the departed person's past or a different role (or activity) in that person's life. The project could be done by a single participant, a couple bereaved persons, or an entire bereaved family.

2. Fabric paint or embroidery could be used as well as special items or mementos stitched onto the cloth squares.

3. When the quilt is finished, a party could occur, inviting family members and friends to come admire the quilt and share stories about the person who is being memorialized.

A BEREAVED PERSON'S DREAM JOURNAL

Intended Participant: Bereaved Person.

1. The bereaved person could create a journal summarizing all of his/her memorable dreams. Dreams in which the departed person appears may be especially noteworthy.

2. After recording the dream, the participant would address in the journal the following three questions:

A. Are there any regrets or unfinished business from the past that is apparent in this dream? What do I need to do in regard to those regrets or that unfinished business?
B. What does this dream say about what I need to be doing now to help me recover from this death?
C. What does this dream tell me about what I need to be doing with the loved ones that still remain in my life?

MY POEMS OF GRIEF

Intended Participant: Bereaved Person.

1. Soon after the death of a loved one, the bereaved person could spend a couple weeks working on a poem that expresses all of his/her sadness. The person should not let a day go by without working on the wording of the poem, trying to accurately express the depth and extent of the sadness. After a couple weeks have passed and the bereaved person has some satisfaction with the accuracy of the poem's expression, he/she could go on to the next poem.

2. The person could then spend a couple weeks working on a poem that expresses all of his/her anger, not letting a day go by without working on the wording of the poem, trying to accurately express the depth and extent of his/her anger. After a couple weeks have passed and the person has some satisfaction with the accuracy of the poem's expression, he/she could go on to the next poem.

3. The person could then spend a couple weeks working on a poem that expresses all of his/her fears, not letting a day go by without working on the wording of the poem, trying to accurately express the depth and extent of his/her fears. After a couple weeks have passed and the person has some satisfaction with the accuracy of the poem's expression, he/she could go on to the next poem.

4. The person could then spend a couple weeks working on a poem that expresses all the joy he/she has received from the person who has died, not letting a day go by without working on the wording of the poem, trying to accurately express the depth and extent of his/her joy. After a couple weeks have passed and

the person has some satisfaction with the accuracy of the poem's expression, he/she could go on to the next, and final, poem.

5. The person would spend a couple weeks working on a poem that expresses how his/her loved one would want the grieving person to live the rest of his/her life, covering physical, emotional, and spiritual goals. Each day would involve some work on the poem, trying to accurately express the goals. After a couple weeks have passed and the person has some satisfaction with the wording of the poem, he/she can proceed to the next, and final step, of this activity.

6. The bereaved person would then find a friend or a counselor who is willing to meet with him or her on five separate occasions to go over each of the five poems, one each meeting. The first meeting would explore the person's sadness, the second would explore anger, the third would explore fears, the fourth would explore the feelings of joy, and the last would explore the physical, emotional, and spiritual goals for the future.

THE ANCIENT STONE CEREMONY

Intended Participant: Bereaved Person.

1. The participant would go to a place where there are many stones. The participant would then draw a six foot wide circle in the dirt.

2. The participant would then stand in the center of the circle and invoke the person who has died to come into the circle and stand beside him/her. The participant would then try to sense this person as being in the center of the circle.

3. The participant would then go out of the circle and find four stones. Each stone would be placed on the edge of the circle, each stone being placed in one of the four directions: south, west, north, and east.

4. From the center of the circle, the participant would face the stone on the south edge of the circle. While facing that stone, the participant would bring to mind the childhood of the person who has died and the childlike qualities of that person. Then the participant would go over to the stone, touch it, and verbalize his/her appreciation for the child in the person who has died.

5. From the center of the circle, the participant would then face the stone on the west edge of the circle. While facing that stone, the participant would bring to mind the brave and courageous qualities of the person who has died. Then the participant would go over to the stone, touch it, and verbalize his/her appreciation for the bravery and courage in the person who has died.

6. From the center of the circle, the participant would then face the stone on the north edge of the circle. While facing that stone,

the participant would bring to mind the skills and talents of the person who has died. Then the participant would go over to the stone, touch it, and verbalize his/her appreciation for the skills and talents of the person who has died.

7. From the center of the circle, the participant would then face the stone on the east edge of the circle. While facing that stone, the participant would bring to mind the vision and dreams of the person who has died. The participant would then go over to the stone, touch it, and verbalize his/her appreciation for the vision and dreams of the person who has died.

8. The participant would then sit down in the center of the circle and thank the person who has died for all the contributions the person has made to the participant's life. The participant would then meditate for awhile upon all the gifts he/she has received from the person who has died.

9. When the participant is ready to leave this place, he/she would return the rocks to their original places, erase the circle, and leave that place the way it was found. In doing this final step, the meditates upon two important realities:

> A. From one point of view, we cannot change time or place. What has happened has happened. Reality is what reality is. When someone has died they are no longer here and will not return.
> B. From another point of view, no thing or no person is completely confined to a particular time or a particular place. I can carry that person with me now wherever I go. That person can now be embodied in me and in everything I witness and experience.

A CAREGIVER'S SPIRITUAL AFFIRMATIONS

Intended Participant: Caregivers.

1. Any of the following affirmations could be repeated verbally or internally each day.

2. Encourage the participant to pick his/her own affirmation.

3. A participant's chosen affirmation could be visibly posted as a physical reminder of the verbal or internal practice, posting the affirmation on a mirror, refrigerator door, or some other frequently visited location.

4. Sample affirmations:

> A. God has chosen my heart, my mind, and my body as vehicles of loving service.
> B. With every act of caring, I am getting closer and closer to God.
> C. I will not fear, for God is with me. I will not despair, for God is with me. I will not tire, for God is with me.
> D. Nothing can defeat me, for my courage and strength come from God.
> E. I receive strength through the comfort of God. I receive comfort through the strength of God.

5. The word "God" is used in these affirmations, but you can substitute "Jesus," "the Revered Buddha," "Allah," "the Goddess," "the Divine Spirit," or any other appropriate wording.

PERCEIVING THE HOLY INCARNATE

Intended Participant: Caregivers

1. The task of caregiving is made easier when it is perceived as spiritual work.

2. As a caregiver, consider the person in your care as an incarnation of the holy. View your work as spending time with the Christ; you are caring for Jesus. View your work as spending time with the Buddha; you are caring for Buddha. As a caregiver, you are working with the Tao, Krishna, Allah, the Goddess, all that is holy.

2. When considering the care recipient as Jesus, you would need to consider this person as fully human and fully divine. When considering this person as the Buddha, you would need to consider this person as being made of the same stuff as the Buddha, the Buddha's human nature and the Buddha's enlightened nature. This person is not like Jesus; this person is Jesus. This person is not like the Buddha; this person is Buddha. All that is holy is in this person.

3. You also need to perceive yourself as the incarnation of the holy. In caring, you are walking with the feet of Jesus. You are reaching out with the arms of the Buddha. You are touching with the hands of Allah. You are speaking with the voice of Krishna. You are showing the love of the Goddess. You are representing the presence of the Tao. In giving care, you are doing holy stuff with holy people.

SHARING THE SILENCE

Intended Participant: Caregivers.

1. Sometimes the best thing we can do is simply share time together in silence, supporting a person simply through our presence.

2. A caregiver should not be quick to end these times. A caregiver should relax, knowing that his/her simple presence can sometimes change a profane world into a holy one.

Guided Imagery For The Imaginative Spirit

Chapter Introduction

In this chapter you will have the opportunity to create many deeply moving personal experiences by tapping into the power of imagination. Whether you work alone or guide someone else through these exercises, you will be amazed at the wealth of meaningful experience that lies within our minds and souls.

Human imagination was described by Albert Einstein as the "eye to the soul." Using our imagination allows us to explore beyond our conscious thoughts and ego defenses. With it we can reach into the vast wisdom of unconscious experience, that which is uniquely ours and that which we share with all humanity. The renown psychotherapist Carl Jung, using a technique he called "active imagination," believed anyone could connect to this deeper unconscious resource for understanding and growth. From it can flow new perceptions of our self, our relationships with others, and deeper understanding of personal and collective experiences.

There are several important considerations before you begin to use these imagery techniques. First prepare a quiet, comfortable, and relaxing setting. Take care to turn off the phone and answering machine. Ask others to respect your privacy and let them know that you do not want to be disturbed. If possible, select a place or room that you associate with quiet, peaceful reflection. Adjust the lighting and temperature to suit your mood. Consider playing soft, soothing, meditative music in the background. Dress in comfortable, loose clothing. When you are ready, assume a supported, but relaxed, body position. This could be in a special chair, or couch, in a soothing bath, on the floor with pillow under your neck, or on a rolling hill or near a quiet stream.

Second, learn to relax your breathing, your physical body, and your mind. You can do this by simple breathing in through you nose and out through your mouth, holding and releasing your breath ever slightly longer until you reach a comfortable level of relaxation. Then take time to focus upon, and relax, your major body parts. Start with your toes, move to your feet, lower legs, thighs, hamstrings, stomach, lower back, upper back, chest, shoulders, arms, hands, fingers, neck, and head. As you focus upon each area, imagine that it is getting warm, loosening up, feeling heavy, feeling calm, and becoming relaxed.

Third, allow your attention to go to your mind and your thoughts. Imagine you are watching your thoughts go by as you would watch a movie go from beginning to end. Notice how your thoughts begin to slow down. If a particular thought continues to demand your attention, tell it that you understand it is important and promise that you'll go back to it later. Set it aside and continue to relax toward a quiet mind.

Fourth, as you review the technique you want to keep in mind that it is just a guide or a map. The true and real experience you'll have comes from inside your mind and your soul, not from adhering to the technique. To let go in this manner requires great flexibility, respect and trust of your inner experience, and a willingness to be vulnerable and open to what your mind may offer you. Do not try to control the experience. Do not question or judge what happens. Let the experience flow. Let it be confusing if it is confusing. Let it be scary if it is scary. Let it be pleasant if it is pleasant. Do not be too concerned with the meaning of what happens while you experience the imagery. The meaning may come to you later or can often be teased out through discussion with a trusted other. Remember that imagery is a healing process and is good no matter where it leads you.

Finally, be careful not to take your imagery experiences too literally. While some literal issues may arise in the course of an exercise, remember that a lot is happening on the psychological, emotional, and spiritual levels that does not necessarily fully fit into your literal experience. Your images will have shape and form, sound and movement, affect and emotion. They may even have taste and smell. The real value of these images is often found in their symbolic meaning. For example, if I imagine my father and I in a fight, it may have less to do with actual anger toward my father but rather may be about my frustration with my own parental judgements of myself.

Our images may help us work on unfinished business. They may help us uncover and express some closely kept emotion. They may motivate some important action. They may help us gain some needed insight. They may help us access or create a meaningful resource that we can use to better cope. No matter what happens, imagery exercises help us get in touch with our self, our heart, our mind, and our soul. Enjoy the journey you are about to take. Let it come to you. If you need any help understanding your imagery experience do not hesitate talking about it with someone you trust.

GUIDED IMAGERY: MY SACRED TEMPLE

Intended Participant: The Sick, Dying, Bereaved, Caregivers, and/or General Public.

1. The following guided imagery could be read to the participant or recorded for the participant's use.

> While in a comfortable position, close your eyes and center your attention upon your feelings. . . . Sense the particular feelings that you have when I say the following words: "peace," . . . "contentment," . . . "freedom," . . . "safety." . . . Now, with those feelings in your consciousness, imagine a special place of retreat made just for you. This is your private, sacred temple. Imagine this place that is characterized by peace, contentment, freedom, and safety. Whatever place comes into your consciousness, stay there in your mind. . . . Do not let other places or thoughts intrude. If they do, keep returning to that place of peace, . . . contentment, . . . freedom, . . . and safety. . . .
>
> Become completely absorbed in this place. . . . Imagine the soothing feelings that permeate your entire body. . . . Imagine the relaxing sounds that you hear in this place of peace. . . . Try to sense the soothing aromas that are present in this place. . . . Examine what is around you. . . . Examine what is below you. . . . Examine what is above you. . . . Examine what you see in the distance. . . . Examine what is close to you. . . . Examine everything that is contributing to your peace, . . . contentment, . . . freedom, . . . and safety. . . .

This is your special place. . . . This place
belongs completely to you, and you may come here
whenever you want to come. . . . Whenever you are
anxious, you may close your eyes and go to this place
of peace, . . . contentment, . . . freedom, . . . and
safety. . . . This is your special place. . . . Once again,
examine this place with all of your senses: the sights, .
. . the sounds, . . . the aromas. . . .

You are about to leave this place. But you
may return whenever you wish. All you need to do is
just close your eyes and travel in your imagination. . .
. For now, say goodbye to the soothing aromas. . . .
For now, say goodbye to all the pleasant sights. . . .
For now, say goodbye to the peace, . . . contentment, .
. . freedom, . . . and safety. . . . Whenever you are
ready, knowing that you can always return, slowly
open your eyes. . . .

2. Discussion or an art project could follow to help capture the
experience.

GUIDED IMAGERY: THE GIFT OF HOLINESS

Intended Participant: The Sick, Dying, Bereaved, Caregivers, and/or General Public.

1. The following guided imagery could be read to the participant or recorded for the participant's use.

>Close your eyes and imagine that you are walking across a vast desert. The desert is hot. . . . The desert is dry. . . . The desert is barren. . . The desert is lonely. . . .
>
>You are lost, without any direction, without any purpose. You feel discontented. You feel uncomfortable. You are alone, without friend or companion. . . .
>
>You realize that there have been many times in your life when you have experienced similar feelings. You realize that there have been many moments when your life felt just like this hot, dry, lonely desert. . . . Perhaps you are now in one of those times when you feel very little purpose, very little contentment, very little companionship. . . .
>
>Be aware of these feelings as you imagine yourself walking across this desert. . . . You feel the hot sun. . . . You trudge through the dry sand. . . . You see the empty horizon. . . . As you are looking at that lonely horizon, you see some gathering clouds way off in the distance. . . . Mighty, billowing, glorious clouds. The clouds are at once gentle and powerful. You know that they are being sent by a loving God. . . . As the clouds come closer, you grow more and more aware that they are God-given clouds, intended just for you. . . . Clouds that are being sent

to bring you some refreshing rain, refreshing rain that will wash away your troubles. . . .

These mighty, billowing clouds are now directly over your head, blocking the hot rays of the sun. . . . From the clouds, a gentle, cleansing rain falls. . . . You turn your face to the sky and feel the raindrops wash your face. . . . The rain washes away all your shortcomings. Every shortcoming that you have ever had is being washed away by this gentle rain. . . . All of your mistakes are being washed away. Every mistake you have ever made is being washed away by this gentle rain. . . .

As the rain falls, you look around and see that the desert is gradually turning into a luxuriant garden. . . . Trees are sprouting up before your eyes and are reaching for the sky. . . . Green grass is growing out of the sand, creating a lush carpet beneath your feet. . . . Flowers, red, yellow, pink, are blossoming around the tree trunks and blooming throughout the green grass. . . .

As the rain gradually stops, you notice the rainwater slowly evaporate from your skin. . . . The clouds are drifting away and revealing a new sun, a pleasantly warm, welcoming sun. A relaxing sun. A God-given sun. . . . You see a rainbow in the sky. . . . You hear birds singing. . . . You see butterflies fluttering among the flowers. . . .

As you breathe in the fresh air, the God-given air, you feel all your burdens being taken away. . . . As you breathe in the fresh, God-given air, you feel your body straightening, your chin rising. You feel proud of who you are. . . . You feel loved just as you are. . . . You feel content just as you are. . . .

The pleasant warmth of the sun cradles you.

The fresh air permeates your body with its freshness. .
. . You are surrounded with warmth. You are
saturated in freshness. . . .Breathe in the pleasant
warmth. . . . Breathe in the freshness. . . . You are
softened with love. . . . You are saturated with love. .
. . You are relaxed with contentment. . . . You are
softened with contentment. . . . You are at peace. . . .
God is fully with you. God will never leave you. . . .

2. Discussion could follow.

GUIDED IMAGERY: THE POWER WITHIN

Intended Participant: The Sick, Dying, Bereaved, Caregivers, and/or General Public.

1. The following guided imagery could be read to the participant or recorded for the participant's use.

Place your body in a comfortable position and close your eyes. . . . Breathe in through your nose and out through your mouth. . . . Relax all the muscles of your body and focus on your thoughts. . . . Slow down the thoughts of the day and allow your mind to focus on a very special place. . . . You are going to be meeting your Power Within, your special companion, your special guide. . . . Imagine the characteristics you would like your guide to have: strength, peace, love, loyalty, kindness, etc. . . . As you await for your guide to appear, notice the beauty of the special place where you are. Notice the colors, . . . the shapes of and distance between objects, . . . the qualities of lightness and shadow. . . . Hear the sounds of your special place. Notice their peaceful, soothing rhythm. . . . Feel what it is like to be there. Notice the temperature, the warmth, and the movement of air or water. . . .

As you continue to take in the wonder of your special place, notice in the distance the form of your guide seemingly approaching you. . . . As your guide comes closer, you notice certain features. . . . Perhaps you recognize your guide as a deceased relative coming to help you, a super hero, an animal, or a spiritual or religious figure. . . . When your guide comes up to you, introduce yourself and explain your

deepest concern. . . . Ask your guide for help with
your concern. . . . Await a response. The response
may be in words, with a feeling, by picture, or
through demonstration. What is your guide's
response? . . . If you are unsure of the meaning of the
response, ask the guide to explain. . . . Sometimes the
guide will take you back to important memories or on
an imaginary trip somewhere else. Where does your
guide want to take you? . . . Go with your guide
wherever you are being taken and know that the
meaning of where you are going may not come to you
right away. Maybe you'll understand it tomorrow,
next week, or sometime later in your life. Go with
your guide wherever you are taken. . . Also ask the
guide for a gift, something symbolic that you can take
with you as you continue to contemplate the meaning
of your experience with the guide. What gift do you
receive? . . . Then thank the guide for the help you
have received. . . . Ask the guide to be available for
you in the future. . . . Then slowly open your eyes and
return to the room. . . . Take a moment to reflect on
your experience. . . .

2. You might want to consider discussing your experience with a
trusted other.

GUIDED IMAGERY:
BREATHING FORGIVENESS, LOVE, AND PEACE

Intended Participant: The Sick, Dying, Bereaved, Caregivers, and/or General Public.

1. The following guided imagery could be read to the participant or recorded for the participant's use.

Close your eyes and concentrate on your breathing. . . . Breathe in and breathe out. . . . Breathe in and breathe out. . . . As you are concentrating on your breathing, bring to your awareness that which is causing you to suffer. . . . Bring to mind the source of your suffering. . . . Bring to mind the anger connected to your suffering. . . . Bring to mind the sadness connected to your suffering. . . . Imagine gently placing all of your suffering inside the very center of your being, in the center of your body. Your suffering is at the very center of your body. . . .

As you are breathing, imagine the air you inhale swirling around that suffering, that suffering that is at the very center of your being. . . . Feel the air that you inhale swirl around your suffering. . . . With each breath you take in, imagine the air swirling around that suffering. . . .

Breathe in the air of forgiveness. . . . Imagine all of that forgiveness swirling around your suffering. . . . Every breath you take in is a breath of forgiveness. . . . Forgiveness moving through your suffering. . . . Breathe in the air of forgiveness. Forgiveness coming to your suffering. . . .

Now, with each breath that you expel, imagine the air moving out from your suffering. It is

the air of forgiveness. . . . You are now breathing out
forgiveness. . . . As you continue to breathe out
forgiveness, make a smile of forgiveness. . . . Breathe
out forgiveness. . . . And smile. . . .

Now with each breath that you take in,
imagine the air swirling around that suffering at the
very center of your being. . . . Breathe in the air of
love. . . . Imagine love swirling around your suffering.
. . . Every breath you take in is a breath of love. . . .
Love moving through your suffering. . . . Breathe in
the air of love. Love coming to your suffering. . . .

Now, with each breath that you expel,
imagine the air moving out from your suffering. . . .
You are now breathing out love. . . . As you are
breathing out love, make a smile of love. . . . Breathe
out love. . . . And smile. . . .

Now, with each breath that you take in,
imagine that the air is once again swirling around
your suffering. . . . Every breath you take in is a
breath of peace. . . . Peace moving through your
suffering. . . . Breathe in the air of peace. Peace
coming to your suffering. . . .

Now, with each breath that you expel,
imagine the air moving out from your suffering. . . .
You are now breathing out peace. . . . As you are
breathing out peace, make a smile of peace. . . .
Breathe out peace. . . . And smile. . . .

You are breathing in forgiveness. . . . You are
breathing out forgiveness. . . . You are smiling the
smile of forgiveness. . . . You are breathing in love. . .
. You are breathing out love. . . . You are smiling the
smile of love. . . . You are breathing in peace. . . .
You are breathing out peace. . . . You are smiling the
smile of peace. . . . There is forgiveness with our

suffering. Forgiveness. . . . There is love with our
suffering. Love. .. . . There is peace with our
suffering. Peace. . . . Forgiveness. . . . Love. . . .
Peace. . . .

2. You might want to consider discussing your experience with a trusted other.

GUIDED IMAGERY: MY LOVING COMPANION

Intended Participant: The Sick, Dying, Bereaved, Caregivers, and/or General Public.

1. The following guided imagery could be read to the participant or recorded for the participant's use.

Close your eyes and concentrate on your breathing. . . . Breathe in and breathe out. . . . Breathe in and breathe out. . . . Imagine yourself standing in an open field, standing there in all of your vulnerability. You are standing as a wounded person, a person without any armor, standing there with all of your hurt, with all of your pain, with all of your disappointment, with all of your sadness. Imagine yourself standing in such a state, standing in the middle of an open field. . . .

As you are standing there, you see in the distance a person coming towards you. This is the most loving person that you can imagine, walking towards you. Imagine the most loving person imaginable walking towards you. . . . You see love pouring out from this person, pouring out towards you. . . . As the person comes up to you and stands before you, you hear these words come from the person's mouth: "I accept you with all of your wounds. . . . I accept you with all of your pain. . . . I accept you with all of your anger. . . . I accept you with all of your sadness. . . . I accept you for all that you are." . . .

Now picture this loving person say to you: "I too am wounded. . . . I too am in pain. . . . Let us hold one another so that we are one." . . .

The two of you come together with arms wrapped around one another. Your arms are softly, very softly, wrapped around one another. . . . Relax in those arms. . . . Your woundedness is accepted. . . . You are loved, . . . even with all of your pain, . . . even with all your anger, . . . even with all of your sadness. . . . You are loved. . . .

Slowly unwrap your arms from one another, and, holding each other's hands, begin slowly walking out of that field. . . . I want you to imagine that you are now walking together into this very room where you find yourself right now, walking over to two chairs that are placed side by side. . . . The two of you sit down, next to one another. . . . This person is seated next to you right now. . . . Imagine this loving person sitting next to you right now, . . . this person who loves you. . . .

Slowly open your eyes. . . .

2. You might want to consider discussing your experience with a trusted other.

GUIDED IMAGERY: FAMILY REUNION

Intended Participant: The Sick, Dying, Bereaved, Caregivers, and/or General Public.

1. The following guided imagery could be read to the participant or recorded for the participant's use.

Close your eyes. Picture yourself standing alone. . . . Imagine your mother walking up to you. . . . Picture her standing in front of you. . . . Listen to your mother as she says, "I love you for all that you have been." "I love you for all that you have been." . . . Listen to your mother saying to you, "I love you for all that you are." "I love you for all that you are." . . . Hear her saying, "I love you for all that you will be." "I love you for all that you will be." . . . Listen to your mother's request: "Forgive me for anything I have done to hurt you." "Forgive me for anything I have done to hurt you." . . . Hear your mother saying, "I forgive you for anything that you have done to hurt me." "I forgive you for anything that you have done to hurt me." . . . Listen to her say, "I love you; I always have; I always will." "I love you; I always have; I always will." . . . Notice how it feels when your mother wraps her arms around you and holds you. . . . Feel her holding you now. . . . Know she will always hold you. . . . Know she will always hold you because she loves you. Know she really does love you. . . .

Now picture yourself standing alone. . . . Imagine your father walking up to you. . . . Picture your father standing in front of you. . . . Listen to your father say, "I love you for all that you have

Page 90

been." "I love you for all that you have been." . . .
Listen to your father saying to you, "I love you for all
that you are." "I love you for all that you are." . . .
Hear your father saying "I love you for all that you
will be." "I love your for all that you will be." . . .
Listen to your father's request: "Forgive me for
anything I have done to hurt you." "Forgive me for
anything I have done to hurt you." . . . Listen to your
father saying, "I forgive you for anything you have
done to hurt me." "I forgive you for anything you
have done to hurt me." . . . Hear your father saying, "I
love you; I always have; I always will." "I love you; I
always have; I always will." . . . Notice how it feels
when your father wraps his arms around you and
holds you. . . . Feel him holding you now. . . . Know
he will always hold you. . . . Know he will always
hold you because he loves you. Know he really does
love you. . . .

Now open your eyes knowing that your
mother loves you and your father loves you. . . .

2. You might want to consider discussing your experience with a
trusted other.

GUIDED IMAGERY: RELIEF FROM PAIN

Intended Participant: The Sick, Dying, Bereaved, Caregivers, and/or General Public.

1. The following guided imagery could be read to the participant or recorded for the participant's use.

> Place your body in a comfortable position. . . . Close your eyes and breathe in through your nose and out through your mouth. . . . Relax all the muscles of your body and allow the thoughts of the day to slow. . . . Imagine yourself preparing to take a soothing bath. Run the water how you like it. . . . Turn down the lights or light a candle. Softly play some relaxing music in the background. . . . Test the water to see if it is just right. If not, adjust it to your liking. . . . Notice near the bath a set of small canisters, each filled with a very special substance meant to reduce a variety of different pains. Some will warm an area. Some will cool an area. Some will relax nerve endings. Some will cause normal feelings to return. Others are completely mysterious with their own secret properties. All have been found to help reduce or eliminate pain. . . .
>
> When you are ready, slowly make your way into the bath. First slide your toes into the water. Feel a tingle on the surface of your skin as the water surrounds your toes. . . . Notice how the warmth slowly soaks into the muscles of your toes. Feel your toes relax. Imagine the warmth flowing into the bones of your toes. Hold the warmth there. Feel your toes relax. . . . Now slide your feet into the water. Notice how the water surrounds you and warms the muscles

and bones of your feet. . . . Slide your legs into the water. Let the warm water soak into the muscles of your legs. Feel your legs loosen and relax. . . . Now slide your body into the water. Feel the warmth surround your waist. . . . Feel the warmth soothing your lower back. . . . Feel the warmth on your stomach. . . . Your upper back. . . . Your chest. . . . Shoulders. . . . Slowly slide your arms into the water and feel the warmth gently relax your arms and hands. . . . Let the warmth flow freely through the skin, into the muscle, and into the bone. . . . Now, notice the steam from the surface of the water. Imagine the steam slowly relaxing and massaging the muscles of your neck, head, and face. . . . Notice how your head is relaxed. . . . As you sit in the bath, soaking up the warmth, listening to the music fading away in the distance, reflect on the kind of pain relief you would like. . . . Without disturbing the water and the rhythm of the relaxed mood, slowly pour one of the special substances into the water. Notice how the substance seems to know just where to go. . . . Let it go to the particular area of your pain. Allow your body to receive it. Take it in. Let the special substance flow freely to the area of pain. Notices how it works, slowly and methodically calming the area, sending special pain relief properties to the area. . . . Let the special substance do its job. . . . Let your mind wander off, wherever it wants to go. Enjoy the experience. Take your time. . . . Relax. . . .

Now, slowly return your attention to the bath. You see another pain control substance called "Total Peace Of Mind." Add this to the bath water. . . . This new substance has a special fragrance, the fragrance of Total Peace Of Mind. Breathe in the fragrance of

Total Peace Of Mind. . . . Feel the warmth of Total
Peace Of Mind. . . . Now, slowly finish your bath. . . .
Slowly return your attention to the room. . . . As you
return, slowly allow movement back in your body. . .
. Remember the feelings you have just experienced
and give them a name. What one word do you give to
your feelings right now? . . . Repeat this word
whenever you want a dose of pain relief. . . . This is
your special word, repeat it whenever you want relief
from pain. . . .

2. You might want to consider discussing your experience with a
trusted other.

GUIDED IMAGERY: ON PEACE

Intended Participant: The Sick, Dying, Bereaved, Caregivers, and/or General Public.

1. The following guided imagery could be read to the participant or recorded for the participant's use.

Get as physically comfortable as you possibly can. Concentrate on the word "relax." Relax. . . . Relax. . . . Relax. . . .

Concentrate on the word "peace." Peace. . . . Peace. . . . Peace. . . .

Imagine the most peaceful location that you can possibly envision. . . . Imagine a very serene place. . . . What does that place look like? . . . Look in all directions at this peaceful place. . . . Relax in this peaceful place. . . .

Now, still keeping your eyes closed, imagine the most pleasant smell that you can possibly imagine. . . . Imagine breathing in this serene fragrance. . . . Relax as you breathe in this calming fragrance. . . .

Now, imagine the most soothing taste that you can possibly imagine. . . . Imagine savoring this pleasant taste. . . . Relax as you experience this peaceful taste. . .

Now, imagine the most relaxing touch that you can possibly imagine. . . . Imagine being caressed and held with this comforting touch, being peacefully caressed and held by someone you love very dearly. . . . Relax as you are gently touched by this person whom you love. . . .

Relax as you see your peaceful scene. . . .

Relax as you smell that soothing fragrance. . . . Relax
as you taste that pleasing taste. . . . Relax as you are
caressed and held with peaceful touch. . . . Relax. . . .
You are at peace. . . . You can relax. . . . Peace. . . .
Peace. . . . Peace. . . .

2. You might want to consider discussing your experience with a
trusted other.

Page 96

GUIDED IMAGERY: THE HOLY WOMAN

Intended Participant: The Sick, Dying, Bereaved, Caregivers, and/or General Public.

1. The following guided imagery could be read to the participant or recorded for the participant's use.

        Close your eyes. . . . Relax. . . . Relax. . . . Relax. . . .
        You have just been granted a special audience with a holy woman named "Rose Of Sharon." Rose Of Sharon is a very famous holy woman, known throughout her homeland of Southern Africa. She is a very knowledgeable woman, said to know things that no other person knows; what others do not know, Rose Of Sharon knows. . . .
        Rose Of Sharon is a very large woman. Her skin is as black and as beautiful as the most precious ebony. Her hair is so thick and full that it is said that there is as many hairs on her head as there are animals on the continent of Africa. Her clothes are said to contain all the colors of the rainbow. Picture Rose Of Sharon. . . . See how large she is. See her black and beautiful skin. . . . See her great head of hair: more hair than animals in Africa. . . . See her robes with all the colors of the rainbow. . . . Look into her eyes and see all her knowledge, great knowledge, knowledge which nobody else has. . . . This is a holy woman. This is a great woman. This is a knowledgeable woman. . . .
        Try in your mind to hear the sounds of the African home of Rose Of Sharon. Try to imagine the sounds of Africa. . . . These are sounds that reach

back to the beginning of time. . . . Hear the sounds of
the bird. . . . Hear the sounds of the elephant. . . .
Hear the sounds of the lion. . . . Hear the sounds of
the water. . . . Hear the sounds of the wind. . . . These
are the sounds of the beginning of time. These are the
sounds that surround this holy woman named Rose Of
Sharon. . . .

Try to imagine the smells of the African
home of Rose Of Sharon. Try to breathe in the smells
of Africa. . . . These smells, like the sounds, take you
back to the beginning of time. . . . Breathe in the
musky scent of Africa. . . . Breathe in the animals. . . .
Breathe in the plants and the trees. . . . Breathe in the
earth and the people. . . . Breathe in the forests and
the deserts. . . . Breathe in all the ancient history of
this place. . . .

Now, in your imagination, visualize Rose Of
Sharon sitting across a fire from you. . . . The flames
penetrate the evening sky. Sparks are flying. Flames
are dancing. . . . Look across the fire into the eyes of
Rose Of Sharon. Look into her all-knowing eyes. . . .
As she looks across at you she tells you that you have
three questions that you may ask her, three questions
that she will answer from the knowledge that she has
that no one else has. . . . She will answer three of your
questions. . . .

Think. What one question do you want
answered more than any other question. . . . What is
the very first question you want to ask Rose Of
Sharon. . . . In your imagination, ask that question to
Rose Of Sharon as she sits across from you. Ask this
holy woman that question. . . .

Imagine the all-knowing Rose Of Sharon
answering your question. Listen to her response. Feel

her message. . . .

You now have another question. What is your second, and next to last, question that you wish to ask Rose Of Sharon? In your imagination, ask her that question. . . .

What answer does Rose Of Sharon give to your second question? Listen to her response. Feel her message. . . .

Now for your last question. This question needs to be special because it is the last question that you will be able to ask the all-knowing Rose Of Sharon. Ask Rose Of Sharon your last question. . . .

What answer does Rose Of Sharon give to your last question? Listen to her response. Feel her message. . .

Now thank Rose Of Sharon. . . . Now, before leaving you feel that you want to give something to Rose Of Sharon, something that shows your appreciation for her answering of your questions. What do you have to offer as a gift of thanksgiving? What do you want to give Rose Of Sharon? . . . Imagine yourself giving this to her, . . . once again thanking her, . . . and turning to leave this place, . . . leaving with your new knowledge. . . .

Now picture where you are right now. Picture the room where you are right now. . . . What can you recall about the room with your eyes closed? Visualize this room. . . .

Now slowly open your eyes. . . .

2. Discussion or an art project could follow to help capture the experience.

GUIDED IMAGERY:
A CHRISTIAN VERSION OF A HOLY CONVERSATION

Intended Participant: A Dying Person.

1. The following guided imagery could be read to the participant or recorded for the participant's use.

> Close your eyes and imagine that you are being transported to Gethsemane. . . . You see Jesus all alone, kneeling and praying. . . . You see his power. You also see his vulnerability. You see all of his internal struggles. No one understands him. He feels alone. He feels unloved. . . . You quietly walk over to his side and kneel next to him. You kneel there in silence. . . . After a short while, Jesus turns to you with love in his eyes and asks, "What can I do for you?" . . . You look Jesus in the eyes and say, "Please tell me how you feel as you are facing death." Listen to Jesus talk about death while he is in Gethsemane. . . . Imagine his words, his tone of voice, his facial expressions. . . . What does Jesus say about death while he is in the garden of Gethsemane? . . .
>
> Now imagine that you are being transported to the foot of Jesus' cross. . . . You see Jesus hanging alone on that cross. He is in great pain. He feels completely deserted. . . . After a while, Jesus sees you standing below him. With love in his eyes, he asks, "What can I do for you?" . . . You look Jesus in the eyes and say, "Please tell me how you feel as you are dying." Imagine how Jesus talks about death as he is hanging on the cross. . . . What does he say about death while he is hanging on that cross? . . .
>
> Now imagine that you are being transported

to the throne of the resurrected Jesus. You see Jesus relieved of all his pain, basking in the glory of God. . . . You quietly approach the throne. You kneel in silence. . . . After a while, Jesus turns to you with love in his eyes and asks, "What can I do for you?" . . . You look Jesus in the eyes and say, "Please tell me how you feel after you have died." Imagine how Jesus talks about death after he has experienced the resurrection. . . . What does Jesus say about death after the resurrection? . . .

2. You might want to consider discussing your experience with a trusted other.

GUIDED IMAGERY:
A NATURALIST VERSION OF A HOLY CONVERSATION

Intended Participant: A Dying Person.

1. The following guided imagery could be read to the participant
or recorded for the participant's use.

> Close your eyes and imagine yourself
> standing before a great oak tree in the middle of the
> season of Summer. This great oak tree towers before
> you with its deep, strong roots, and its branches
> reaching out in all directions, each branch lavishly
> decorated with thousands of green leaves. . . . Look
> with wonder upon this mighty, richly decorated oak
> tree, this oak tree with many leaves. . . . You see that
> this tree has survived for many generations and has
> witnessed much throughout its years. . . . After you
> have examined this oak tree for a little while, a gentle
> voice comes from the center of its huge trunk, asking,
> "What can I do for you?" . . . You look at this great
> oak tree and say, "Please tell me how you feel in the
> midst of this Summer." Imagine how this oak tree
> would describe its Summer condition. . . .
> Now imagine that you are standing before
> this mighty oak tree in the middle of the season of
> Autumn. Its leaves are glorious and multicolored.
> Most of its leaves are still on the tree, but many have
> fallen to the ground. . . . Look at this tree at the height
> of its beauty and the waning of its liveliness. . . . After
> you have examined this oak tree in this stage of
> transition, a beautiful voice comes from the center of
> its trunk, asking, "What can I do for you?" . . . You
> look at this great oak tree and say, "Please tell me

how you feel in the midst of this Fall." Imagine how
this oak tree would describe its Fall condition. . . .
   Now imagine that you are standing before
this mighty oak tree in the middle of the season of
Winter. Its branches are bare; there are no more
leaves. Several branches have been broken by an ice
storm and lie scattered on the ground beneath the tree.
. . . Look at this tree that has been stripped of all its
beauty, standing in all of its vulnerability, shivering in
the harsh winter wind. . . . After you have examined
this oak tree in this stage of devastation, a quivering
voice comes from the center of its trunk, asking,
"What can I do for you?" . . . You look at this great
oak tree and say, "Please tell me how you feel in the
midst of this Winter." Imagine how this oak tree
would describe its Winter condition. . . .
   Now imagine that you are standing before
this mighty oak tree in the early part of the season of
Spring. Little buds are sprouting all over its branches.
Singing birds have returned to its branches and greet
the tree with encouraging song every morning. . . .
Look at this tree as it witnesses new life around it,
upon it, and within it. . . . After you have examined
this oak tree in this stage of rebirth, an excited voice
comes from the center of its trunk, asking, "What can
I do for you?" . . . You look at this great oak tree and
say, "Please tell me how you feel in the midst of the
Spring." Imagine how this oak tree would describe its
Spring condition. . . .

2. You might want to consider discussing your experience with a
trusted other.

GUIDED IMAGERY:
A BUDDHIST VERSION OF A HOLY CONVERSATION

Intended Participant: A Dying Person.

1. The following guided imagery could be read to the participant or recorded for the participant's use.

Close your eyes and imagine yourself meeting Gautama in his youth, before he had ever witnessed suffering, before he had ever witnessed death. Imagine him in his protected environment, removed from all hardships and pain, isolated within his wealthy family's compound. . . . Look upon this protected, innocent youth named Gautama. . . . This young man turns to you and asks, "What can I do for you?" . . . You look at him in all his innocence and say, "Please tell me how you feel at this time in your life." Imagine how Gautama would describe this time of his life. . . .

Now imagine yourself meeting Gautama when he first discovers suffering and death. Imagine his shock at discovering pain for the very first time. . . . Look upon this shocked and disturbed young man, this man whose protected world has just been dramatically challenged by the existence of pain and death. . . . This now disturbed young man turns to you and asks, "What can I do for you?" . . . You look at him and say, "Please tell me how you feel at this time in your life." Imagine how Gautama would describe his discovery of pain and death. . . .

Now imagine yourself meeting the Buddha just as he has gotten up from sitting under the bodhi tree. Imagine his whole being aglow with the realization of enlightenment. . . . Look upon the Buddha, this man who has now become aware of the way to overcome suffering, the way to transcending pain and death. . . . The Buddha turns to you and asks, "What can I do for you?" . . . You look at the Buddha in the glow of his enlightenment and say, "Please tell me how you see death." Imagine how the Buddha would describe his enlightened perspective of death. . . .

2. You might want to consider discussing your experience with a trusted other.

GUIDED IMAGERY: HEALING EXPERIENCE

Intended Participant: A Dying Person.

1. The following guided imagery could be read to the participant or recorded for the participant's use.

Place your body in a comfortable position. Close your eyes and breathe deeply in through your nose and out through your mouth. Feel the natural relaxation that comes through simply focusing upon your breathing. . . . Relax all the muscles of your body and focus on your thoughts. . . . Slow down the thoughts of the day and imagine that you have just arrived in a "holy" place. Notice what you see, the colors and objects around you. This is a holy place. . . Notice what you hear. The sounds close to you and the sounds far away. This is a holy place. . . Feel the atmosphere of this place. . . . Imagine that your body is in a physical position of direct contact with all the holy power of this place. Feel the light of this power cast upon you, bathing you in holy light. . . . Feel the sounds of this power reverberate within you. Feel the holiness of the power course throughout your body. . . . You may feel a tingle, a warmth, or some other sensation of healing. Let it go to the places within you that especially need it. You are being healed with holiness. . . .
　　　　Imagine the holy power of this place giving you all that you need. If it's relief from pain: feel relief from pain. If it's a lifting of your spirits: feel them uplifted. If it's reassurance and faithfulness: feel reassurance and faithfulness. . . . Whatever the healing you seek, feel the power of this place helping

you achieve it. . . . As you are sensing this healing, let
a short prayer, mantra, or meaningful phrase come to
your mind. What meaningful phrase comes to mind? .
. . Repeat that phrase and know that when you say it,
you can once again have the healing of this place with
you. . . .

2. Discussion or an art project could follow to help capture the
experience.

GUIDED IMAGERY: DEATH IMAGERY

Intended Participant: The Sick, Dying, Bereaved, Caregivers,
and/or General Public.

1. The following guided imagery could be read to the participant
or recorded for the participant's use.

> Place your body in a comfortable position.
> Close your eyes and breathe deeply in through your
> mouth and out through your nose. . . . Relax all the
> muscles of your body and focus on your thoughts.
> Slow down the thoughts of the day until you feel a
> peaceful quietness in your mind. . . . Now visualize
> within your mind the person who has caused you the
> most amount of pain in your life. What person has
> caused you the most amount of pain in this life? . . .
> Focus upon this person. Notice the person's body,
> face, and eyes. . . . Notice the feelings that emerge.
> Let all these feelings flow out of you. They float out
> of your body and up into the sky. All your feelings
> towards this person are floating away from you, going
> up into the sky. . . . Say goodbye to these feelings as
> they float away up into the sky. . . . Now say goodbye
> to this person in front of you. . . . Now imagine
> standing before you the person who has given you the
> most amount of pleasure in your life. What person
> has given you the most amount of pleasure in this
> life? . . . Focus upon this person. Notice the person's
> body, face, and eyes. . . . Notice the feelings that
> emerge. Let all these feelings flow out of you. They
> float out of your body and up into the sky. All your
> feelings towards this person are floating away from
> you, going up into the sky. . . . Say goodbye to these

feelings as they float away up into the sky. . . . Now
say goodbye to this person in front of you. . . .
Now in your imagination visualize yourself as
an infant. . . . Remember all the special experiences
you had in being an infant. Feel them again. . . . Now
let those feelings go. Let them flow out of you. They
float out of your body and up into the sky. All your
feelings about your infancy are floating away from
you, going up into the sky. . . . Say goodbye to your
infancy. . . . Now visualize yourself as a child.
Remember your childhood. Remember all the special
experiences of being a child. Feel them again. . . .
Now let those feelings go. Let them flow out of you.
They float out of your body and up into the sky. All
your feelings about your childhood are floating away
from you, going up into the sky. . . . Say goodbye to
your childhood. . . . Now visualize yourself in early
adulthood. Remember your adulthood. Remember all
the special experience of being an adult. Feel them
again. . . . Now let those feelings go. Let them flow
out of you. They float out of your body and up into
the sky. All your feelings about your adulthood are
floating away from you, going up into the sky. . . .
Say goodbye to your adulthood. . . . Now visualize
yourself now. Remember all the special experiences
of recent times. Feel them now. . . . Now let those
feelings go. Let them flow out of you. They float out
of your body and up into the sky. All your feelings
about your current life are floating away from you,
going up into the sky. . . . Say goodbye to your
current life. . . .
Now imagine your own death. . . . Feel the
flow of your life energy leaving your body, being
pulled down by gravity. . . . Notice the stillness of

your lungs, heart, and muscles. . . . Let yourself pass.
. . . Leave behind your body, your clothes, your
possessions, and the physical aspect of your
relationships. . . . Experience your death state, your
death consciousness, and your bodiless state. . . . Let
your mind, soul, and body, take in the experience. . . .
Now you may gradually return your life
energy to your body. You are coming back to the
world of the living. . . . Feel your body once again
with all the life energy that is in it. Feel the life energy
flowing through your veins. . . . Feel the life energy
swirling through your body. . . . Breathe in the breath
of life. Deep breaths. Life-giving breaths. . . . Now
slowly open your eyes and remember what you want
to remember. Forget or push back that which you
choose to forget. You are alive again. Very alive. . . .

2. You might want to consider discussing your experience with a
trusted other.

GUIDED IMAGERY: MY FUNERAL

Intended Participant: The Sick, Dying, Bereaved, Caregivers, and/or General Public.

1. The following guided imagery could be read to the participant or recorded for the participant's use.

Lying down on a floor, close your eyes and try to make your body as quiet as you possibly can. . . . Relax deeply. . . . Relax until you feel as though your body and the floor are one. . . . Your life has left you. Only your body remains on the floor. . . .

Your body no longer moves. Your body is dead. Your physical being is gone. . . . Only your consciousness survives and your consciousness realizes that it is the day of your funeral. . . .Your funeral is about to begin. . . .

You see your body lying in a casket at the end of a funeral parlor. Picture the lid open on your casket and see your dead body lying inside. . . . Notice how you appear. . . . Notice how you have been preserved. Notice what you are wearing. . . .

See the people who have come to your funeral. Look around at who has come. Recognize the individuals. Look into their faces. . . . Notice their expressions. . . . Notice their emotions. . . . Notice those who are mingling with others. . . . Notice those who are silent and reserved. . . .

Imagine people coming up to the casket one at a time. Who is the first person who comes up to your casket? . . . How does this person react to seeing your body? . . . What would you like to say to this person? Remember you are dead and cannot say

anything. . . . Notice the second person who comes up
to your casket. What reactions does this person have?
. . . What do you want to say to this person? How do
you feel being unable to say those words? . . . Who is
the next person to look at your body? How does this
person react? . . . What thoughts do you have about
this person? . . .

Looking around, is there someone missing
that you hoped would be there? . . . Who is the
missing person? . . . What has caused this person to
be absent? . . . What would you like to say to that
person? . . .

Notice your emotions as you picture your
funeral? . . . Focus on those feelings. . . . Experience
your feelings. What do you feel? . . .

Notice the music that is playing at your
funeral. . . . Listen to the music as it is being played. .
. . Is the music what you wanted to hear? . . .

Notice the flowers at your funeral. . . . Are
there many? Are there few? . . . Visualize and smell
the flowers at your funeral. . . . How do you feel
about these flowers? . . .

Notice who is getting up to give your eulogy.
. . . Listen to what this person says. . . . How do you
feel as you listen? . . .

The funeral is now ending and the people are
leaving. . . . Notice how people look as they are
leaving the service. . . . Prepare yourself to leave the
service and to return to your body. . . .

Now take your attention back to your present
physical body, the live body, the body that is laying
on the floor this very moment. . . . Feel the weight of
your head. . . . Feel the weight of your pelvis. . . . Feel
your heels. . . . Feel your upper body. . . . Feel your

upper body move as you take in each breath. . . . Feel
the life-giving air enter your body, allowing its life-
giving energy to swirl throughout your entire body. . .
. You are alive! . . . Your life is not over yet! . . . You
have more time. What do you want to do with this
time? . . . What did you learn from imagining your
funeral? . . . What do you need to do? Who do you
need to talk to? . . .

Slowly open your eyes. . . .

2. You might want to consider discussing your experience with a
trusted other.

GUIDED IMAGERY: RELEASING YOUR LOVED ONE

Intended Participant: The Bereaved.

1. The following guided imagery could be read to the participant or recorded for the participant's use.

Close your eyes and feel the coolness of each breath that you inhale. . . . Feel the coolness in your lungs. . . . Notice the freshness of the air. . . . Feel the freshness as you inhale. . . . Notice how the cool freshness soon turns to warm heaviness. . . . Feel the warmth of the air in your lungs. . . . Feel the heaviness as you exhale. . . . Feel the warmth and heaviness of the air as you exhale. . . . Feel the cool freshness coming in and the warm heaviness going out. . . .
Picture in your mind the most loving person that you can possibly imagine. Picture this most loving person standing in front of you. . . . Imagine this person's arms stretched out toward you. . . .
Imagine that there are hundreds of people standing in a line behind this loving person. The line of people extends very far into the distance, and disappears into the glow of a warm and peaceful light. You see this long line of hundreds of people disappear into that warm and peaceful light. . . .
In your arms, you are carrying someone who has died, someone with whom you have felt great love. The body hardly has any weight at all. . . . You're looking at this person in your arms, this person who has died, this person you have loved. . . . You are reminded of some special moments you had with this person. Picture in your mind a few of those special moments. . . . Look once again at this person

Page 114

in your arms. . . . Remember and say goodbye. . . .
Now you carry the body you are holding over
to the loving person with outstretched arms. Then
gently place the dead body in the outstretched arms. .
. . Notice how the loving person turns and places the
body in the arms of the next person in the line and
you watch the body being passed along the line of
people from one to another toward the glowing, warm
and peaceful light. The body is gently and carefully
passed from one person to another to another to
another. . . . The body is finally passed into that
glowing light. You see the light become brighter and
warmer and more peaceful as the body enters the
light. . . . You know that the body is now safe, very
safe, very very safe. . . .
You look once again at the loving person
across from you. That person shares a warm and
accepting smile and says, "Thank you. Your friend is
safe now, very safe. So, it is okay for you to go now."
. . . You turn around and begin walking away from
this special place. As you are leaving, you once again
become aware of your breathing. . . .
Feel the coolness and freshness of each breath
that you inhale. . . . Feel the warmth and heaviness of
each breath that you exhale. . . . Feel the freshness
come in and the heaviness go out. . . . Your friend is
safe. . . . You are experiencing great relief. . . . Your
friend is safe. . . . You feel peaceful. . . . Your friend
is safe. . . . You are relieved. . . .

2. You might want to consider discussing your experience with a
trusted other.

Meditations
For The Contemplative Spirit

Chapter Introduction

In this chapter meditations are given for contemplation. These meditations are given to assist a participant in developing a healthy mental attitude. One, two, or several quotations are presented for the subject matter of the meditation. With each of these meditations, the following steps could be followed:
1. The participant could use the quotations for daily meditation. A specific time each day might be set aside for that meditation.
2. Each meditation could involve reading the quotations (aloud or silently) three times with five minutes of reflection after the three-fold repetition.
3. The participant might then want to write down some thoughts in a journal after the completion of each daily meditation.
4. When the participant believes that little more can be gained from a particular meditation, another meditation might be used.

A MEDITATION ON
GROWING IN THE MIDST OF SUFFERING

Intended Participant: The Sick, Dying, Bereaved, Caregivers, and/or General Public.

Here are the quotations for the meditation:

A. "Affliction comes to us all, not to make us sad, but sober, not to make us sorry, but wise, not to make us despondent, but by the darkness to refresh us." - Henry W. Beecher.

B. "Mishaps are like knives, that either serve us or cut us, as we grasp them by the blade or handle." - James Russell Lowell.

C. "The art of living lies less in eliminating troubles than in growing with them." - Bernard Baruch.

A MEDITATION ON THE PURPOSE OF SUFFERING

Intended Participant: The Sick, Dying, Bereaved, Caregivers, and/or General Public.

Here are the quotations for the meditation:

A. "Very often what nourishes our spirit most is what brings us face to face with our greatest limitations and difficulties." - Jack Kornfield.

B. "Character cannot be developed in ease and quiet. Only through experience of trial and suffering can the soul be strengthened, vision cleared, ambition inspired and success achieved." - Helen Keller.

C. "There is no birth of consciousness without pain." - Carl Jung.

D. "It is the darkest nights that prepare the greatest dawns." - Sri Aurobindo.

A MEDITATION ON PATIENCE

Intended Participant: The Sick, Dying, Bereaved, Caregivers, and/or General Public.

Here are the quotations for the meditation:

A. "Patience is all the strength a man needs." - Sathya Sai Baba.

B. "Patience is the best remedy for every trouble." - Plautus.

C. "Patience conquers everything in the end." - Paramananda.

A MEDITATION ON FAITH

Intended Participant: The Sick, Dying, Bereaved, Caregivers, and/or General Public.

Here are the quotations for the meditation:

A. "For truly I say to you, if you have faith as a mustard seed, you shall say to this mountain, 'Move from here to there,' and it shall move; and nothing shall be impossible to you." - Jesus.

B. "Faith heals, faith creates, faith works wonders, faith moves mountains." - Sivananda.

C. "By faith you can move mountains; but the important thing is not to move mountains, but to have faith." - Arthur Clutton-Brock.

A MEDITATION ON PRAYER

Intended Participant: The Sick, Dying, Bereaved, Caregivers, and/or General Public.

Here are the quotations for the meditation:

A. "Prayer is not flight; prayer is power. Prayer does not deliver a man from some terrible situation; prayer enables a man to face and to master a situation." - William Barkley.

B. "Let us not pray to be sheltered from dangers but to be fearless in facing them. Let us not beg for the stilling of the pain but for the heart to conquer it. - Rabindranath Tagore.

A MEDITATION ON DYING

Intended Participant: A Dying Person and/or A Caregiver of Dying Person.

Here are the quotations for the meditation:

A. "O man, do not be afraid of death at all. Thou art immortal. Death is not the opposite of life. It is only a phase of life. Life flows on ceaselessly. The fruit perishes but the seed is full of life. The seed dies but a huge tree grows out of the seed. The tree perishes but it becomes coal which has rich life. Water disappears but it becomes the invisible steam which contains the seed of new life. The stone disappears but it becomes lime which is full of new life. The physical sheath only is thrown but life persists." - Sivananda.

B. "Do not allow death to disturb you, do not let the demise of flesh be the cause of pain or anguish. It is merely riddance of your vehicle, the sloughing off of your clothes." - Shantidasa.

C. "To be afraid of death is like being afraid of discarding an old worn-out garment. - Mohandas Gandhi.

D. "Death is no more traumatic than taking off an old coat." - Eknath Easwaran.

A CAREGIVER'S MEDITATION ON CHANGING PEOPLE

Intended Participant: A Caregiver of Sick Person, Caregiver of
Dying Person, or Caregiver of Bereaved Person.

Here are the quotations for the meditation.

A. "It is useless and futile to try to change other people.
The only person I can change is myself." - William
Curtiss.

B. "He who expects to change the world will be
disappointed; he must change his view. When this is
done, the tolerance will come, forgiveness will come and
there will be nothing he cannot bear." - Hazrat Inayat
Khan.

C. "You are not here to change the world, the world is
here to change you." - Shantidasa.

A CAREGIVER'S MEDITATION ON
UNCONDITIONAL ACCEPTANCE

Intended Participant: A Caregiver of Sick Person, Caregiver of Dying Person, or Caregiver of Bereaved Person.

Here are the quotations for the meditation:

A. "The willingness to allow [care recipients] to be themselves by supporting them with our presence is essential. In the spiritual realm, presence implies an 'unconditional acceptance' of people." - Patrice O'Connor.

B. "Acceptance means that there are no reservations, conditions, evaluations, and judgments of [a person's] feelings, but rather a total positive regard for the [person] as a person of value. . . . It is not acceptance up to this or that point and no further, but acceptance even though the [person] possesses values, attitudes, and feelings different from our own." - Angelo Boy and Gerald Pine.

C. "I accept the patient as being in an okay space except for the ways the patient defines as unsatisfactory." - Sheldon Kopp.

A CAREGIVER'S MEDITATION
FOR CENTERING UPON THE OTHER

Intended Participant: A Caregiver of Sick Person, Caregiver of Dying Person, or Caregiver of Bereaved Person.

Here are the quotations for the meditation:

A. "In our best moments as helpers, we encourage clients to look inside for the wisdom to make healthy choices. . . . To do this, we must resist our impulses to provide them with all the answers, to point out what they are doing wrong, and to single-handedly meet all their needs." - Dale Larson.

B. "Our work . . . would change remarkably if we thought about it as ongoing care rather than as the quest for a cure." - Thomas Moore.

C. "When our agenda is to fix or cure, the focus is on ourselves as 'ego-heroes.' . . . In caring, the helper never becomes the focus of the experience." - Carol Montgomery.

A CAREGIVER'S MEDITATION
ON NOT BEING A MESSIAH

Intended Participant: A Caregiver of Sick Person, Caregiver of Dying Person, or Caregiver of Bereaved Person.

Here are the quotations for the meditation:

A. "Many people are caught in the Messiah Trap. . . . Messiahs try to be helpful wherever they go. . . . By saying 'No!' to the Messiah Trap, you allow others to take responsibility for their own lives and for the development of their own self-esteem." - Carmen Renee Berry.

B. "I have nothing to give another; but I have a duty to open him to his own life, to allow him to be himself - infinitely richer than he could ever be if I tried to enrich and to shape him only from the outside." - Michel Quoist.

A CAREGIVER'S MEDITATION
ON ELICITING THE OTHER'S STRENGTH

Intended Participant: A Caregiver of Sick Person, Caregiver of
Dying Person, or Caregiver of Bereaved Person.

Here are the quotations for the meditation:

A. "No one wishes to be 'rescued' with someone else's
beliefs. Remember your task is not to convert anyone to
anything, but to help the person in front of you get in
touch with his or her own strength, confidence, faith, and
spirituality, whatever that might be." - Sogyal Rinpoche.

B. "The truest help we can render an afflicted man is not
to take his burden from him, but to call out his best
strength that he may be able to bear the burden." -
Phillips Brooks.

A CAREGIVER'S MEDITATION ON NON-INTERFERENCE

Intended Participant: A Caregiver of Sick Person, Caregiver of Dying Person, or Caregiver of Bereaved Person.

Here is the quotation for the meditation:

"There are many situations where you as helper <u>do</u> solve the problem in the sense that you provide a medication, share some specific information, teach a skill, or massage a sore back. This kind of active assistance is necessary and vital in caregiving; sometimes it is all that is needed. But when we look at emotional difficulties, interpersonal dilemmas, treatment decisions, and other psychosocial problems, the appropriateness of the patient as problem-solver becomes more clear-cut. Here, even though you are active and may even teach skills or offer educational input, the responsibility for change remains with the client." - Dale Larson.

A CAREGIVER'S MEDITATION ON LISTENING

Intended Participant: A Caregiver of Sick Person, Caregiver of Dying Person, or Caregiver of Bereaved Person.

Here is the quotation for the meditation:

> "I suspect that the most basic and powerful way to connect to another person is to listen. Just listen. Perhaps the most important thing we ever give each other is our attention." - Rachel Naomi Remen.

A CAREGIVER'S MEDITATION ON CLINICAL DISTANCE

Intended Participant: A Caregiver of Sick Person, Caregiver of Dying Person, or Caregiver of Bereaved Person.

Here is the quotation for the meditation.

> "The more you think of yourself as a 'therapist," the more pressure there is on someone to be a 'patient.' The more you identify as a 'philanthropist,' the more compelled someone feels to be a 'supplicant.' The more you see yourself as a 'helper,' the more need for people to play the passive 'helped.' You're buying into, even juicing up, precisely what people who are suffering want to be rid of: limitation, dependency, helplessness, separateness." - Ram Dass.

A CAREGIVER'S MEDITATION ON EDUCATION

Intended Participant: A Caregiver of Sick Person, Caregiver of Dying Person, or Caregiver of Bereaved Person.

Here are the quotations for the meditation:

A. "All of our training is not only useless, it's damaging." - Sheldon Kopp.

B. "Learn your theories as well as you can, but put them aside when you touch the miracle of the living soul." - Carl Jung.

A CAREGIVER'S MEDITATION ON ROLE PLAYING

Intended Participant: A Caregiver of Sick Person, Caregiver of
Dying Person, or Caregiver of Bereaved Person.

Here is the quotation for the meditation:

"Learning how to be yourself is one of the greatest
challenges you face as a helper. If you don't play at roles
and you are real, honest, and authentic in your helping
relationships, you will have more success and less stress
as a caregiver." - Dale Larson.

A CAREGIVER'S MEDITATION ON
HAVING A GENTLE PRESENCE

Intended Participant: A Caregiver of Sick Person, Caregiver of Dying Person, or Caregiver of Bereaved Person.

Here are the quotations for the meditation:

A. "When we honestly ask ourselves which persons in our lives mean the most to us, we often find that it is those who, instead of giving much advice, solutions or cures, have chosen rather to share our pain and touch our wounds with a gentle and tender hand. The friend who can be silent with us in a moment of despair or confusion, who can stay with us in an hour of grief and bereavement, who can tolerate not-knowing, not curing, not-healing and face with us the reality of our powerlessness, that is the friend who cares." - Henri Nouwen.

B. "Sometimes our best service to those we love is to simply stand by, be silent, be patient, be hopeful, be understanding, and wait." - Leo Buscaglia.

A CAREGIVER'S MEDITATION ON KINDNESS

Intended Participant: A Caregiver of Sick Person, Caregiver of Dying Person, or Caregiver of Bereaved Person.

Here are the quotations for the meditation:

A. "My religion is kindness." - The Dalai Lama.

B. "Be the living expression of God's kindness — kindness in your face, kindness in your eyes, kindness in your smile, kindness in your warm greeting." - Mother Teresa.

C. "There are three rules of dealing with those who come to us: (1) Kindness, (2) Kindness, (3) Kindness." - Fulton J. Sheen.

A CAREGIVER'S MEDITATION ON BEING HAPPY

Intended Participant: A Caregiver of Sick Person, Caregiver of Dying Person, or Caregiver of Bereaved Person.

Here is the quotation for the meditation:

> "Happiness is Inherent. Happiness is Immediate. Happiness is most Obvious." - Da Free John.

A CAREGIVER'S MEDITATION ON SMILING

Intended Participant: A Caregiver of Sick Person, Caregiver of Dying Person, or Caregiver of Bereaved Person.

Here are the quotations for the meditation:

A. "We shall never know all the good that a simple smile can do." - Mother Teresa.

B. "A tiny bud of a smile on our lips nourishes awareness and calms us miraculously. . . . Our smile will bring happiness to us and to those around us." - Thich Nhat Hanh.

A CAREGIVER'S MEDITATION ON CRYING

Intended Participant: A Caregiver of Sick Person, Caregiver of Dying Person, or Caregiver of Bereaved Person.

Here are the quotations for the meditation:

A. "If tears begin to well up in your eyes, let them come. They will communicate to your family member or friend that you care deeply. Your tears will also give permission to your loved one that he or she can cry as well without feeling uneasy." - Leonard Felder.

B. "Each time we cry, we emerge with clearer eyes, cleaner vision." - Leo Buscaglia.

C. "What soap is for the body, tears are for the soul." - Jewish Proverb.

A CAREGIVER'S MEDITATION
ON SERVICE AS SPIRITUALITY

Intended Participant: A Caregiver of Sick Person, Caregiver of Dying Person, or Caregiver of Bereaved Person.

Here are the quotations for the meditation:

> A. "Life is best spent in alleviating pain, assuaging distress, and promoting peace and joy. The service of man is more valuable than what you call 'service of God.' God has no need of your service. Please man, you please God." - Sathya Sai Baba.

> B. "There is no higher religion than human service. To work for the common good is the greatest creed." - Albert Schweitzer.

> C. "Service of God consists in what we do to our neighbor." - Leo Baeck.

> D. "They serve God well, who serve his creations." - Caroline Norton.

A CAREGIVER'S MEDITATION
ON THE IMPORTANCE OF SERVICE

Intended Participant: A Caregiver of Sick Person, Caregiver of Dying Person, or Caregiver of Bereaved Person.

Here are the quotations for the meditation:

A. "The purpose of life is not to be happy — but to matter, to be productive, to be useful, to have it make some difference that you lived at all." - Leo Rosten.

B. "When people are serving, life is no longer meaningless." - John Gardner.

C. "Fear not that your life shall come to an end; rather fear that it will never have a beginning." - St. John Cardinal Newman.

D. "Let us endeavor so to live that when we come to die even the undertaker will be sorry." - Mark Twain.

A CAREGIVER'S MEDITATION ON SERVICE AS JOY

Intended Participant: Caregiver of Sick Person, Caregiver of
Dying Person, or Caregiver of Bereaved Person.

Here is the quotation for the meditation:

> "I slept and dreamt that life was joy.
> I awoke and saw that life was service.
> I acted and behold, service was joy." - R. Tagore.

A CAREGIVER'S MEDITATION ON MUTUAL HEALING

Intended Participant: A Caregiver of Sick Person, Caregiver of Dying Person, or Caregiver of Bereaved Person.

Here are the quotations for the meditation:

> A. "At a certain point 'helper' and 'helped' simply begin to dissolve. What's real is the helping — the process in which we're all blessed, according to our needs and our place at the moment. How much we can get back in giving! How much we can offer in the way we receive!" - Ram Dass.

> B. "In a true healing relationship, both heal and both are healed." - Rachel Naomi Remen.

> C. "Those whom we support hold us up in life." - Marie Ebner von Eshenbach.

Page 142

A CAREGIVER'S MEDITATION ON SELF-CARE

Intended Participant: A Caregiver of Sick Person, Caregiver of Dying Person, or Caregiver of Bereaved Person.

Here are the quotations for the meditation:

A. "For so much of my life I was run by this nagging voice in the back of my head that kept insisting, 'You're not doing enough! You're not doing enough!' But now I'm starting to listen to my body a lot more. It needs tender loving care and I'm the only one who can provide that. Even though I always feared that if I took better care of myself it would mean I'd become selfish or self-indulgent, I've discovered that's not the case." - Leonard Felder.

B. "Nothing may be more important than being gentle with ourselves. . . . We learn the value of recognizing our limits, forgiving ourselves our bouts of impatience or guilt, acknowledging our own needs. We see that to have compassion for others we must have compassion for ourselves." - Ram Dass.

C. "When you make choices for your own growth, . . . you also make opportunities for others to grow as well." - Carmen Renee Berry.

Prayers For The Willful Spirit

Page 144

Chapter Introduction

Sometimes caregivers can feel awkward when approached to say prayers by their care recipients. Yet, oftentimes the people for whom they are caring strongly desire to receive prayers. How might caregivers respectfully respond to such prayer requests?

One way to not respond is to say, "Let me go get someone who is professionally trained in that area." That is a disrespectful response. That is disrespectful because you were asked to pray for them. Finding someone else to do the job is avoiding their request, not respecting it.

So, how can caregivers respectfully respond to such a request? Here are six possible respectful responses. (One particular response might be most comfortable for you. Or a particular situation might make one more appropriate than another. However, do not use the response "Let me go get someone else.")

1. One way of responding respectfully is very direct. First ask, "What would you like me to pray for, and how would you like me to pray?" Then adjust your prayer to what they say. That's a respectful response.

2. Another way is to first say, "I appreciate your request. However, before I begin, do you mind if I pray in the way that I'm accustomed to?" By saying that first before you begin your prayer, you are alerting this person that maybe their expectations of what you deliver might be very different from what you actually deliver. (They're Southern Baptist and you're Roman Catholic, and they think you're Southern Baptist. Or, they're Christian and you're Jewish, and they might think you're Christian.) - That's a respectful response: before praying, get permission to pray in your accustomed way.

3. A third way to respond respectfully is to give a generic prayer. The only thing that divides faith communities on the issue

of prayer is simply how we begin and how we end our prayers. The middle is always the same. I know what that middle is by analyzing the question: I know three things about anyone who asks the question "Will you pray for me?" even if I do not know that person's faith. (1) I know that person obviously believes that there is some kind of power in praying. That person would not be asking for something that didn't do anything. (2) That person is not asking me to give a meditation on the spring time; that person wants a prayer that directs that power specifically towards him/her. (3) That person has a particular need driving him/her to ask for that prayer. Now, all I need to know is the need (I do not need to know the faith) in order to pray with that person. For I can internally begin and internally conclude and externally share the common center.

[Example: Willard grabs my arm and says, "Will you pray for me?" I do not know Willard's faith, but I do know he's experiencing a lot of anxiety. So I internally begin (as I normally do). Then I verbally share the common center: "I am asking that Willard might find comfort and peace. And as I am praying for Willard, I sense that he has available to him, both within and around him, comfort and peace. And as I am praying, I sense that Willard has that awareness as well. May that awareness grow this day and in the days ahead, so that tomorrow and the next day Willard might have more comfort and more peace. And as I am praying, I know that it will be so. And I give thanks that it is." And then internally I can conclude. (Whether I say "in the name of the Father, the Son, and the Holy Spirit" or "praise be to Jesus" or "praise be to Allah" or "praise be to the Goddess.") I have thus respectfully responded to Willard's request by sharing the common center to prayer that I know he shares with me.]

4. A fourth way to respond respectfully is to say, "Let's pray together. You begin and I'll follow." Then you can adjust your contribution to how he/she begins.

5. A fifth way: "Let's pray together in silence. I will be praying for you. I would appreciate you praying for me." That's respectful.

6. "I have you now, and I will keep you in, my thoughts and my prayers."

Any of these responses are respectful, much more respectful than saying, "Let me go get someone else."

The following prayers can be used with people of various spiritual traditions. They can also be altered to fit specific traditions. Whether using these prayers for yourself or for someone else, please feel free to alter the wording to fit the particular situation.

PLEA FOR INTERVENTION
(For the Sick, Dying, Bereaved,
their Caregivers, and/or General Public.)

That which is Light, please shine in my darkness.
That which is Goodness, please deliver me from my evil.
That which is Wisdom, please educate me in my ignorance.
That which is Power, please lift me out of my weakness.

PRAYER IN THE MIDST OF DOUBT
(For the Sick, Dying, Bereaved,
their Caregivers, and/or General Public.)

Am I talking to myself?
Who could I be speaking to if not myself?
I think I am asking if there might be something more than what I
can touch, see, or measure.
I want there to somehow be some principle or force of caring at
the center of this universe.
I want there to be something more.
Something more!
Please!
Listen!
Speak!
Care!

PRAYER FOR ONENESS WITH GOD
(For the Sick, Dying, Bereaved,
their Caregivers and/or General Public.)

God's thoughts must be filtered through a human brain.
God's love must flow through a human heart.
God's will must be portrayed through a human spirit.
God's pain must be felt in a human body.

Let my brain know the thoughts of God.
Let my heart beat with the love of God.
Let my spirit be driven by the will of God.
And, even though my body might feel some of the pain of God
      let me believe that God's thoughts are always with me,
      God's love is always for me, and God's will always
      seeks my greatest good.

THE PRAYER OF NO FEAR
(For the Sick, Dying, Bereaved,
their Caregivers, and/or General Public.)

In the beginning, there was God.
Today, there is God.
Tomorrow, there will be God.

Before today, God was with me.
During this day, God is with me.
If I am here tomorrow, God will be with me then as well.

If this is in fact so, and I do believe it, how can I have any fear?
Why would I ever be afraid of anything?
What worries could I ever have?

PRAYER FOR GUIDANCE
(For the Sick, Dying, Bereaved,
their Caregivers, and/or General Public.)

Creator of light, please give me guidance.
Creator of mountains, please give me strength.
Creator of lakes, please give me serenity.

Creator of me, please open me up to receive You,
With all of Your guidance,
With all of Your strength,
With all of Your serenity.

REMIND ME THAT I AM IMMERSED IN LOVE
(For the Sick, Dying, Bereaved,
their Caregivers, and/or General Public.)

Flowers and candy are strange expressions of love.
Love expresses itself best in the midst of pain and suffering.
Love expresses itself best in the midst of doubt, depression, and
    sadness.
Love expresses itself best in the midst of anger and chaos.
Love expresses itself best in the midst of open sores and human
    waste.
Perhaps I get no flowers or candy, but that does not mean that I
    am not immersed in love.

Remind me that I am immersed in love.
Remind me that I am immersed in love.
Remind me that I am immersed in love.

HELP ME TO LEARN THAT HOLINESS IS EVERYWHERE
(For the Sick, Dying, Bereaved,
their Caregivers, and/or General Public.)

Help me to learn that this is a holy moment.
Help me to learn that this is a holy place.
Help me to learn that holy people are all around me.
Help me to learn that I am also holy.

Help me to learn that holiness is everywhere.
Holiness is everywhere.
Holiness is everywhere.

LOVE IS EVERYWHERE
(For the Sick, Dying, Bereaved,
their Caregivers, and/or General Public.)

Love has been with me.
Love will be with me.
Love is over me.
Love is under me.
Love is to the right of me.
Love is to the left of me.
Love is within me.
Love surrounds me.

HELP ME RECEIVE HELP
(For the Sick, Dying, and Bereaved)

Help me receive help from others.

Help me, in my sorrow, to receive the joy of others.
Help me, in my weakness, to receive the strength of others.
Help me, in my pain, to receive the comfort of others.
Help me, in my anxiety, to receive the peace of others.
Help me, in my loneliness, to receive the love of others.

Help me receive help from others.

BLESSED ARE THOSE
(For the Sick, Dying, and Bereaved)

Blessed are those who come into my presence.
Blessed are those who listen to my truth.
Blessed are those who hear my doubts.
Blessed are those who see my anger.
Blessed are those who sense my pain.
Blessed are those who witness my tears.
Blessed are those who hold my body.
Blessed are those who will not turn away.

HELP ME CONVINCE MYSELF
(For the Sick, Dying, and Bereaved)

Help me convince myself that I am worth loving.
Help me convince myself that these hands are worth holding.
Help me convince myself that others want to look into my eyes.
Help me convince myself that I am worth loving.

PERCEIVING THE WONDERFUL
(For the Sick and Dying)

I give thanks for perceiving the wonderful.

I look up into the heavens and see a vast array of planets and
      stars, and I know that the world is wonderfully made and
      the subject of Your wonderful love.
I see the intricacies of a single snowflake and hear of the
      intricacies of a single cell, and I know that the world is
      wonderfully made and the subject of Your wonderful
      love.

Though my heart is weak,
      I perceive that I am wonderfully made and the subject of
      Your wonderful love.
Though my lungs are tired,
      I perceive that I am wonderfully made and the subject of
      Your wonderful love.
Though my muscles are sore,
      I perceive that I am wonderfully made and the subject of
      Your wonderful love.
Though my bones ache,
      I perceive that I am wonderfully made and the subject of
      Your wonderful love.
Though my emotions are drained,
      I perceive that I am wonderfully made and the subject of
      Your wonderful love.

I give thanks for perceiving the wonderful.

FOR PEACE, COMFORT, STRENGTH, AND COURAGE
(For the Sick)

May my mind think of peace.
May my lungs breathe in comfort.
May my heart beat with strength.
May my blood flow with courage.

Peace, comfort, strength, courage:
May they be mine.
May I get them.
May I give them.
May I live them.

MAY MY LAST BE MY BEST
(For the Dying)

May my final chapter be my best chapter.
May my last season be my best season.
May my last act be my best act.
May my last breath be my best breath.

PRAYER OF SURRENDER
(For the Dying)

Lead me from individuality to mutuality.
Lead me from despair to hope, from fear to trust.
Lead me from death to Life.
Lead me from myself to You.

MY DYING PRAYER
(For the Dying)

All that is precious in my life is fading away.
The heart that I have been given is tired.
The mind that I have been given is clouded.
The body that I have been given is weak.

I look back and have regrets and wish forgiveness.
May I be forgiven for the people I have hurt.
May I be forgiven for the time I have spent unwisely.
May I be forgiven for the love I have failed to express.

In the life that I have left, may I be determined to not hurt anyone
    else.
In the life that I have left, may I be determined to spend my time
    wisely.
In the life that I have left, may I be determined to express all my
    love.

PRAYER FOR COURAGE
(For the Dying)

I pray for a peaceful death, but if there be no peace, please let me
  have courage.
I pray for a death without pain, but if there be pain, please let me
  have courage.
I pray for a death where there is no disfigurement, but if there be
  disfiguring, please let me have courage.
I pray for a good death, but if it be not good, please let me have
  courage.

PRAYER IN THE MIDST OF LONELINESS
(For the Dying)

I long for a kind word.
I long for a listening ear.
I long for a comforting hand.
I long for a warm embrace.
I long for a gentle kiss.
Help me in my longings.
Help me in my loneliness.
Let me not feel so lonely anymore.
Help me.

I believe there is some help available to me and that is why I
       pray.
I believe there is some strength available to me and that is why I
       pray.
I believe there is some comfort available to me and that is why I
       pray.
Let it be.
Let it be.
Let it be.

I GIVE THANKS
(For the Dying)

I give thanks.
I give thanks.
In the midst of my suffering, I give thanks for all gifts of
    comfort.
In the midst of my despair, I give thanks for all gifts of hope.
In the midst of my darkness, I give thanks for all gifts of light.
In the midst of the bitter taste of my dying, I give thanks for
    every sweet taste of life.
I give thanks.
I give thanks.

PRAYER IN THE MIDST OF FEAR
(For the Dying)

Things are happening to my body and mind that have never
    before happened and I am afraid.
I am facing things that are uncertain and unknown and I am
    afraid.
People are saying that I might die soon and I am afraid.
I am afraid.
Help me with my fear.
I am afraid.
Help me.

I believe there is some help available to me and that is why I
    pray.
I believe there is some strength available to me and that is why I
    pray.
I believe there is some comfort available to me and that is why I
    pray.
Let me have help.
Let me have strength.
Let me have comfort.

PRAYER IN THE MIDST OF PAIN
(For the Dying)

Help me when I feel there can be no help.
When medicine is inadequate, help me.
When technology fails, help me.
When nothing people say or do brings comfort, help me.
Help me.
Help me to bear what often seems unbearable.
Help me.
Help me when I feel there can be no help.
Help me.

I believe there is some help available to me and that is why I
        pray.
I believe there is some strength available to me and that is why I
        pray.
I believe there is some comfort available to me and that is why I
        pray.
Let me have help.
Let me have strength.
Let me have comfort.

WHEN ALL IS DONE
(For the Dying)

Because a meal is over, is the nourishment that it gave nullified?
Because we have finished reading a book, has the skill of the
      author been erased?
Because a day has ended, are its bountiful gifts any less?

Why then should I, at the conclusion of my life, question its
      value?

Help me to discover what nourishment I have bestowed upon
      others.
Help me to see the skills I have offered this world.
Help me to realize the gifts I have given.

PRAYER OF MOURNING
(For the Bereaved)

I pray for all of us who mourn.
May we face each day with courage, strength, and hope.
May nothing destroy what we have been given.
May nothing erase our memories of joy.
May all the good of the past overpower the fear of the future.
May our current laments of grief eventually change into prayers
      of thanksgiving.
I pray for all of us who mourn.

PRAYER OF LAMENT
(For the Bereaved)

A hand I used to hold, I hold no more.
A voice I used to hear, I hear no more.
A fragrance I used to smell, I smell no more.
A smile I used to see, I see no more.

The love I used to know, I know no more.
My senses are deprived.
I am empty.
May my emptiness somehow be filled.

May my emptiness somehow be filled.
Please fill my emptiness.

I WILL ALWAYS REMEMBER
THE BEAUTY OF OUR LOVE
(For the Bereaved)

Just as all seasons have beauty,
So it has been in the seasons of our love.

I will always remember the beauty in the spring of our love.
I will always remember the beauty in the summer of our love.
I will always remember the beauty in the fall of our love.
I will always remember the beauty in the winter of our love.

We have been together in love.
We are together in love.
We will always be together in love.

I give thanks for your love.
I give thanks for God's love.

I give thanks for love.
I will always remember the beauty of our love.

DEDICATION PRAYER
(For Caregivers)

May this prayer be Your prayer.
May my deliberations be Your deliberations.
May my feelings be Your feelings.
May my intentions be Your intentions.
May my resolutions be Your resolutions.
May my actions be Your actions.

A CAREGIVER'S MORNING PRAYER
(For Caregivers)

As I begin this new day, let me have the courage and strength to
      face what lies ahead.
Let me practice tolerance and patience.
Let me reveal empathy and love.
Let me offer sustenance and hope.
And, let me have the wisdom to know when I need to step
      forward and when I need to step back.

I ask all of this so that when I come to the end of this day, I might
      rest having known that my time and energy have been
      wanted and needed.
Yes, I am asking all of this for my own sake, but I am also asking
      for the sake of another.

A CAREGIVER'S EVENING PRAYER
(For Caregivers)

I give thanks for the courage and strength that has carried me
through this day.
I give thanks for whatever tolerance and patience I have been able
to practice.
I give thanks for whatever empathy and love I have been able to
reveal.
I give thanks for whatever sustenance and hope I have been able
to offer.

I give thanks at the conclusion of this day and into this night for
having been needed and wanted.
Let me rest with a thankful body, mind, and spirit.
Let me rest so that I might greet tomorrow with renewed courage
and strength.
I give thanks for rest.

SEEING THE HOLY
(For Caregivers)

Let me see all that is Holy in this person who is before me.
In holding this person's hand, may I realize that I am holding
    Your hand.
In feeding this person, may I realize that I am feeding You.
In washing this person, may I realize that I am washing You.
In giving this person my love, may I realize that I am giving my
    love to You.

PRAYER FOR JOY
(For Caregivers)

May we remember only joy.
May we seek only joy.

May we receive only joy.
May we give only joy.

May joy be within us.
May joy be around us.

May our next moment be filled with joy.
May our last moment be filled with joy.

May joy be always with me.
May joy be always with you.

RECEIVING THROUGH GIVING
(For Caregivers)

May my self-esteem grow through providing others with self-
esteem.
May my strength be founded upon building the strength of
others.
May my fulfillment come in bringing fulfillment to whoever is in
my care.
May whatever I receive be based upon whatever I give.

RECEIVING MORE THROUGH GIVING MORE
(For Caregivers)

In giving strength, I receive strength.
In giving comfort, I receive comfort.
In giving peace, I receive peace.

In touching another, I am touched.
In holding another, I am held.
In loving another, I am loved.

SHARING THE BOUNTY
(For Caregivers)

Giver of peace, may I be a giver of Your bounty.
Contributor of comfort, may I be a contributor of Your bounty.
Provider of strength, may I be a provider of Your bounty.
Guarantor of hope, may I be a guarantor of Your bounty.

WHATEVER I HAVE
(For Caregivers)

Although I may not have the strongest of hands, I offer whatever
    I have for Your service.
Although my feet might not be the most steady, I offer whatever I
    have for Your service.
Although I may not have the most loving of hearts, I offer
    whatever I have for Your service.
Although my mind might not be the most astute, I offer whatever
    I have for Your service.
Although I may not have abundant energy, I offer whatever I
    have for Your service.
Although my soul might not be the most peaceful, I offer
    whatever I have for Your service.
Although I may not have the most determined of wills, I offer
    whatever I have for Your service.
Please receive whatever I have.
I am in Your service.

MAY IT BE ENOUGH
(For Caregivers)

May the strength that I have be enough so that I might give
    strength to another.
May the comfort that comes to me be enough so that I might give
    comfort to another.
May the love that I have found be enough so that I might give
    love to another.
May the hope that I discover be enough so that I might give hope
    to another.

PROPER PERSPECTIVE
(For Caregivers)

Help me to not have any false self-importance
So that I might always know what truly is important.

Help me to laugh at myself
So that I might always be amused.

Help me to see all my foibles
So that I might always be entertained.

Help me to not have any false self-importance
So that I might always know what truly is important.

HELP ME TO REMEMBER
(For Caregivers)

Help me to remember that there is little I need to say and a lot I need to hear.

Help me to remember that I have little to teach and a lot to learn.

Help me to remember that sometimes the most important thing I can give is simply my presence, and sometimes nothing more is even wanted.

Help me to remember that all my education, all my training, and all my experience must always be secondary to my presence.

Help me to remember that I must accept and reaccept and reaccept and reaccept the uniqueness of the individual before me.

Help me to remember that I am not here for me: I am here for another.

BEFORE AN OPERATION: A PRAYER FOR MY PATIENT
(For Caregivers)

Strengthen _____ to do what he (she) has to do and bear
what he (she) has to bear; that, accepting the skills and gifts of
surgeons and nurses, he (she) may be restored to health with a
spirit of thanksgiving. Grant this strength. Grant this acceptance.
Grant this restoration. Grant this thanksgiving. Confidently I
pray.

FOR RELIEF FROM PAIN: A PRAYER FOR MY PATIENT
(For Caregivers)

I am praying for the relief of pain. I ask that the pain which
_____ feels might be lightened. Lighten the pain. Soften
the hard feelings. Ease the suffering. Bring comfort. Bring
respite. Bring relief. As I pray, the pain is being soothed.
Comfort is coming. Respite is coming. Relief is coming.
_____ is feeling the comfort as it comes. _____ is
feeling the relief as it comes. A lightening. A softening. An
easing. Comfort. Respite. Relief. It is happening as I pray.

FOR STRENGTH, JOY, AND COMFORT:
A PRAYER FOR MY PATIENT
(For Caregivers)

I ask that in the midst of weakness, strength might be found. I pray that in the midst of sorrow, joy might be found. I pray that in the midst of pain, comfort might be found. Give _____ strength. Give _____ joy. Give _____ comfort. As I pray for _____, I sense the welling up of strength. I sense the welling up of joy. I sense the welling up of comfort. May this strength, joy, and comfort continue to build. Let it be.

FOR SANCTIFICATION: A PRAYER FOR MY PATIENT
(For Caregivers)

I pray that _____ may become fully aware of the presence of all holy powers. May those powers continue to grow in him (her). _____, you are being touched by the Holy. _____, you are being held by the Divine. _____, you are being fully surrounded by all powers of sanctification. As I pray, this is all coming into being. Let it be now and always.

PRAYER OF DEDICATION
(For Caregivers)

Open sores and human waste,
Sadness and anger,
Frustration and depression,
Physical pain and emotional suffering:
The compost for the planting of my beautiful garden.
My work.
My mission.
My calling.

MY LIMITS AND MY HEALTH
(For Caregivers)

Help me to learn that there is knowledge I cannot have.
Help me to understand that there are things I cannot do.
Help me to know that there are burdens I cannot bear.
For in discovering my limits, I keep my health.
And, in keeping my health, I can be of service to others.

GIVING THANKS FOR MY HARD WORK
(For Caregivers)

I give thanks for the gift of my tears.
I give thanks for my muscle aches.
I give thanks for the gift of my sweat.
I give thanks for my anger.
I give thanks for the gift of my doubts.
I give thanks for my despair.

These are the confirmations of my hard work.
Without these my growth is limited.
Without these my service is suspect.
These are the confirmations of my hard work.

FOR YOU AND FOR ME
(For Caregivers)

To hold another is to hold ourselves.
To heal another is to heal ourselves.
To love another is to love ourselves.
To forgive another is to forgive ourselves.
To abandon another is to abandon ourselves.

THE QUIET AND THE LOUD
(For Caregivers)

May my feet walk gently in your world.
May my hands touch softly on your skin.
May my voice speak sweetly to your ears.
And may my love rattle your bones, blow your mind, and cause
      your spirit to soar.

ONLY THE GOOD
(For Caregivers)

May my will want only the good.
May my mind think only the good.
May my eyes see only the good.
May my ears hear only the good.
May my mouth speak only the good.
May my hands do only the good.

Bibliography

Albom, M. (1997). Tuesdays With Morrie. New York: Doubleday.

Anderson, H. (1989). "After the diagnosis: An operational theology for the terminally ill." Journal of Pastoral Care, 40(2): 141-150.

Anderson, V.C. (1991). Prayers Of Our Hearts In Word And Action. New York: Crossroad.

Attig, T. (1983). "Respecting the dying and bereaved as believers." Newsletter of Forum for Death Education and Counseling, 6(11): 11-16.

Boersler, R.W., and H.S. Kornfeld. (1995). Life to Death. Rochester, VT: Healing Arts Press.

Buber, M. (1947). Tales Of The Hasidim. New York: Schocken Books.

Burns, S. (1991). "The spirituality of dying." Health Progress, 5: 48-54.

Canda, E. (1988). "Spirituality, religious diversity, and social work practice." Social Casework, 69, 238-247.

Carfagner, R. (1990). "A spirituality for the helping professions." Journal of Pastoral Care, 14(1): 61-65.

Carson, V., and K. Huss. (1979). "Prayer: An effective therapeutic and teaching tool. Journal of Professional Nursing and Mental Health Services, 3: 34-37.

Cassidy, S. (1991). Sharing the Darkness. New York: W. W. Norton.

Chapin, T.J. (1987). "Help with hypnosis in the grieving process." Hypnotherapy Today.

Chapin, T.J. (1990). "The power within: A humanistic transpersonal imagery technique. Journal of Humanistic Psychology, 29(4): 444-456.

Childs-Gowell, E. (1992). Good Grief Rituals: Tools for Healing: A Healing Companion. New York: Station Hill Press.

Clinebell, H. (1995). Counseling for Spiritually Empowered Wholeness. New York: Haworth Pastoral Press.

Deloria, V., Jr. (1994). God Is Red: A Native View Of Religion. Golden, CO: Fulcrum Publishing.

Deming, B. (1984). We Are All Part Of One Another. (J. Meyerding, Ed.). Gabriola Island, BC: New Society Publishers.

Doka, K. (1983). "The spiritual needs of the dying patient." Newsletter of Forum for Death Education and Counseling, 6(11), 2-3.

Doka, K. (1993). Living with Life-Threatening Illness. New York: Lexington.

Doka, K. (Ed.) (1993). Death and Spirituality. Amityville, NY: Baywood Publishing.

Dossey, L. (1993). Healing Words: The Power of Prayer and the Practice of Medicine. San Francisco: Harper.

Droege, T.A. (1992). The Healing Presence: Spiritual Exercises for Healing, Wellness, and Recovery. San Francisco: Harper.

Duff, K. (1993). The Alchemy Of Illness. New York: Pantheon Books.

Fadiman, J., & Frager, R. (1997). Essential Sufism. Edison, NJ: Castle Books.

Feinstein, D., and P. E. Mayo. (1990). Rituals for Living and Dying. San Francisco: HarperCollins.

Fichter, J. (1981). Religion and Pain. New York: Crossroads Press.

Ford-Grabowsky, M. (1995). Prayers For All People. New York: Doubleday.

Frankl, V. (1984). Man's Search for Meaning. New York: Washington Square Press.

Hay, M.W. (1989). "Principles in building spiritual assessment tools." American Journal of Hospice Care. 6(5): 25-31.

Heider, J. (1986). The Tao Of Leadership. New York: Bantam.

Highfield, M., & C. Carson. (1983). "Spiritual needs of patients: Are they recognized?" Cancer Nursing, 6(3), 187-192.

Hover, M. (1986). "If a patient asks you to pray with him." RN, 49(4), 17-18.

Irish, D.P. (Ed.). (1993). Ethnic Variations In Dying, Death, And Grief. Washington, DC: Taylor & Francis.

Johnson, C.J., & McGee, M.G. (Eds). (1991). How Different Religions View Death and Afterlife. Philadelphia: The Charles Press.

Kabat-Zinn, J. (1994). Wherever You Go, There You Are. New York: Hyperion.

Kalweit, H. (1992). Shamans, Healers, and Medicine Men. Boston: Shambhala.

Kapleau, P. (1989). The Wheel of Life and Death. New York: Doubleday.

Kramer, K.P. (1988). The Sacred Art Of Dying. New York: Paulist Press.

Kreinheder, Albert. (1991). Body And Soul: The Other Side Of Illness. Toronto: Inner City Books.

Kushner, H. (1981). When Bad Things Happen To Good People. New York: Schocken.

Larson, D.G. (1993). The Helper's Journey. Champaign, IL: Research Press.

Levine, S. (1982). Who Dies? New York: Anchor Books.

Longaker, C. (1997). Facing Death and Finding Hope. New York: Doubleday.

Lynn, J., & Harrold, J. (1999). Handbook For Mortals. New York: Oxford University Press.

Magida, A.J., & Matlins, S.M. (Eds.) (1999). How To Be A Perfect Stranger. (Vols 1 & 2). Woodstock, VT: Skylight Paths Publishing.

McGaa, E. (1990). Mother Earth Spirituality. San Francisco: Harper.

McIntee, J.D. (1998). To Comfort And To Honor. Minneapolis: Augsburg.

Mead, F. (Ed). (1976). The Encyclopedia Of Religious Quotations. Old Tappan, NJ: Fleming H. Revell.

Metrick, S.B. (1994). Crossing The Bridge. Berkeley, CA: Celestial Arts.

Millison, M.B., & J.R. Dudley. (1992). "Providing spiritual support: A job for all hospice professionals." The Hospice Journal, 8(4), 49-65.

Moore, T. (1992). Care of the Soul. New York: HarperCollins.

Nabe, C. (1989). "Health care and the transcendent." Death Studies, 13: 557-565.

New American Standard Bible. (1973). Lockman Foundation. New York: Collins World.

Nouwen, H.J.M. (1972). The Wounded Healer. Garden City, NY: Doubleday.

Nouwen, H.J.M. (1995). Our Greatest Gift: A Meditation on Dying and Caring. San Francisco: Harper.

Oxford Book Of Prayer, The. (1985). (G. Appleton, Ed.). New York: Oxford University Press.

Parkes, C.M. (Ed.) (1996). Death and Bereavement Across Cultures. New York: Routledge.

Pema Chodron. (1991). The Wisdom Of No Escape. Boston: Shambhala.

Ram Dass, & Gorman, P. (19 85). How Can I Help?. New York: Alfred A. Knopf.

Reisz, H.F., Jr. (1992). "A dying person is a living person: A pastoral theology for ministry to the dying." The Journal of Pastoral Care, 46(2): 184-192.

Remen, R.N. (1996). Kitchen Table Wisdom. New York: Riverhead.

Riemer, J. (Ed.). (1996). Jewish Insights of Death and Mourning. New York: Schocken.

Rogers, C.R. (1961). On Becoming A Person. Boston: Houghton Mifflin.

Rosenthal, T. (1974). How Could I Not Be Among You? New York: George Braziller.

Roth, N. (1990). The Breath Of God. Cambridge, MA: Cowley Publications.

Sharp, J. (1997). Living Our Dying: A Way to the Sacred in Everyday Life. New York: Hyperion.

Singh, K.D. (1998). The Grace In Dying. San Francisco: HarperCollins.

Smith, D.C. (1993). "Exploring the religious-spiritual needs of the dying." Counseling and Values, 37(2): 71-77.

Smith, D.C. (1994). The Tao of Dying. Washington, D.C.: Caring Publications.

Smith, D.C. (1995). "Psycho-palliation and the enlightened counselor." Counseling and Values, 39(3), 209-217.

Smith, D.C. (1997). Caregiving: Hospice-Proven Techniques For Healing Body And Soul. New York: Macmillan.

Smith, D.C. (1997). "The litany of release." The Journal of Pastoral Care, 55(4): 431-434.

Smith, D.C. (1999). Being A Wounded Healer. Madison, WI: Psycho-Spiritual Publications.

Sogyal Rinpoche. (1992). The Tibetan Book of Living and Dying. New York: HarperCollins.

Spiro, H.M., McCrea Curnen, M.G., & Wandel, L.P. (Eds.) (1996). Facing Death. New Haven, CT: Yale University Press.

Starhawk. (1997). The Pagan Book of Living and Dying: Practical Rituals, Prayers, Blessings, and Meditations on Crossing Over. San Francisco: Harper.

Stoll, R.I. (1979). "Guidelines for spiritual assessment." American Journal of Nursing, 79: 1574-1577.

Page 184

Tanakh. (1988). New York: Jewish Publication Society.

Teaching of Buddha, The. (1966). Bukkyo Dendo Kyokai. Tokyo: Toppan Printing.

Ten Principal Upanishads, The. (1937). Shree Purohit Swami and W.B. Yeats (Trans.). New York: Collier Books.

Tomlinson, G. (Ed). (1991). Treasury Of Religious Quotations. Englewoods, NJ: Prentice Hall.

Wald, F. (Ed.) (1986). Proceedings from a Colloquium: In Quest of the Spiritual Component of Care for the Terminally Ill. New Haven: Yale University School of Nursing.

Wald, F.A. (1989). "The widening scope of spiritual care." The American Journal of Hospice Care, 6(4), 40-44.

Way of Lao Tzu, The. (1963). Wing-Tsit Chan (Trans.). Indianapolis: Bobbs-Merrill.

Weenolsen, P. (1996). The Art of Dying. New York: St. Martin's Press.

Wegela, K.K. (1996). How To Be A Help Instead Of A Nuisance. Boston: Shambhala.

Weisman, A.D. (1984). The Coping Capacity. New York: Human Sciences Press.

Wilcock, P. (1997). Spiritual Care of Dying and Bereaved People. New York: Morehouse Publishing.

Doug Smith's Seminars

Doug does several seminars for health care employees and the general public. Among those seminars are the following:

"Exploring and Enhancing Spirituality: How to Care for the Spiritual Needs of the Sick, Dying, and Bereaved."

"Final Rights: Caring for People in the Final Phases of Life."

"Putting the Care Back into Health Care."

"Being a Wounded Healer: How to be a Caring and Effective Helper."

For more information on Doug's seminars, you can contact him by phone (608) 231-1541 or by e-mail dougcsmith@juno.com. Or you can learn more about his seminars, including ones that might be already scheduled in your area, by calling Carondelet Management at the American Academy of Bereavement at (800) 726-3888.

Comments on Doug's Seminars

"Beyond any doubt, this was the most inspiring workshop I have ever attended in over forty years as a professional nurse." - Marilyn Kopriva, Nurse, Londonderry, NH.

"This is the ONLY seminar I've ever attended where 100% of my attention was on the speaker 100% of the time. - Jessie Wrinn, Health Care Administrator, Greenville, SC.

"Doug is an absolutely dynamic speaker. You feel "a part of" his words, stories, and expressions. . . . I am so glad I came today. . . . Would love to spread your messages to the world." - Sabrina Russer-Clarq, Psychologist, Rochester, NY.

"The whole seminar: phenomenal! Doug is such a life-affirming speaker. He inspires, motivates, made me laugh — brought me a quiet joy! Made me question myself without guilt or blame. Yippee!" - Kathy Rindock, Social Worker, Allentown, PA.

"I have never been so moved. . . . This speaker is a master when it comes to touching hearts." - Eileen Wrzesniewski, Nurse, Philadelphia, PA.

"This speaker has authenticity, empathy, and unconditional positive regard! - Paul Mathew, Physician, Houston, TX.

Doug Smith's Other Books

The Tao of Dying by Doug Smith
Caring Publishing (c1997)
ISBN: 0-962836-39-7
This book contains a group of meditations for caregivers of the
dying. The meditations are accompanied by photographs by
Marilu Pittman. The book can be ordered through most
bookstores, at www.barnesandnoble.com or www.amazon.com,
or through Centering Corporation at (402) 553-1200.

Caregiving by Douglas Smith
Macmillan Publishing (c1997)
ISBN: 0-02-861663-4
This book contains tools and techniques for working with the
dying. The book centers around addressing various rights of the
terminally ill (the right to be in control, the right to touch and be
touched, the right to laugh, etc.). It can be ordered through most
bookstores, at www.barnesandnoble.com or www.amazon.com,
or through Centering Corporation at (402) 553-1200.

Being A Wounded Healer by Douglas Smith
Psycho-Spiritual Publications (c1999)
ISBN: 0-9672870-0-6
This book is about the author's struggles with several wounds in
his life (death of his daughter, being a patient in a mental
hospital, losing his priesthood, etc.). The book presents a
"spiritual model" of care to complement the "medical model."
The medical model seeks to eliminate wounds; the spiritual
model seeks to find meaning and value in the midst of
woundedness. This book can only be ordered through Centering
Corporation at (402) 553-1200 or through www.amazon.com.

Copies Of This Book

Copies of <u>Spiritual Healing</u> can be purchased at Doug's seminars
at www.amazon.com, or through the Centering Corporation.

Centering Corporation
1531 N. Saddle Creek Rd.
Omaha, NE 68104

Phone: (402) 553-1200
Fax: (402) 553-0507

Email: J1200@aol.com
Website: www.Centering.Org